Table of Contents

Dedication

This book is dedicated to Arlen, Dru, and Fi
and to the memory of Miguel and Eunie.

-    Miko

Acknowledgments

The first edition of this book was not possible without the help of several people who contributed time, resources, and effort so that this piece of work will become a reality. Special thanks to

> Fr. Francisco Estepa, SVD, university president and Dr. Jemma J. Jay, dean of the College of Business and Accountancy, and then accountancy chair Mr. Henry Labasan, CPA

> The review panel, Dr. Eddie Babor (+) of the publications department, Mr. Ramon Boloron of the English department, and to Mr. Danilo Tabaranza, CPA of the accountancy department

> Ms. Marilou Epe-Sale, Mr. Frank Lorenzo Pizarras, CPA and Ms, Arlen Salgados-Canares, CPA all of Step Up Consulting and Creannovate Publishing House

> Students in Accounting 1.n some 8 years back when this book was tested for the first time.

In the production of this revised edition, I would also like to thank Florita Dote-Acero, chair of Accountancy at Holy Name University for encouraging the completion of this work. I also would like to thank the students who have used the first edition of this book for their positive comments.

Michael P. Canares, CPA
Author

Accounting for Non-Accountants
A Work-Text for Basic Accounting

Published by Creannovate Publishing House
Tagbilaran City, Bohol, Philippines
4 June 2018

ISBN 978-621-95672-1-3

Introduction

This book, the revised edition of the first one published in 2011, remains as an answer to the need for a customized textbook for basic accounting students; students who need to acquire accounting knowledge but do not have to go through the kind of preparatory training needed by those who will be taking the CPA board exams. This also is a suitable material for those who would like to learn the basic concepts of accounting and bookkeeping. While there is no substitute to classroom instruction, this book can be also used as a personal learning material by those who want to become bookkeepers or those managers who want to learn how to read their financial statements and understand the financial health of their businesses.

However, the primary purpose of this material is to be a textbook. Thus, the discussions here are made to guide classroom teaching. Each of the chapter is organized in three parts. The first part is the presentation of learning objectives, where the expected learning outcomes of students are presented. This is followed by a theoretical and practical discussion of the concepts briefly described in the chapter title. The final part is the activity section where exercises are presented. The exercises after each chapter are composed of three sets; (1) discussion questions to trigger analysis which can be done either individually or as a group, (2) objective questions to test knowledge and comprehension (and in some chapters problems to test higher order thinking skills), and (3) group activities to enhance learning. The answers to part (2) are available on request to teachers teaching the subject using this textbook.

<u>Chapter 1: Businesses and the Need for Financial Information</u> discusses the reasons why businesses exist, how businesses are organized, and how important is financial information to be able to manage businesses well. The chapter discusses the reasons why businesses are set up, the types of business organizations, and the functions of management that will be impacted by financial information.

<u>Chapter 2: Role of Accounting in Business</u> presents the basic definition of accounting, the general accounting process, the five basic accounting values, and the fundamental assumptions used in accounting for business transactions. In this chapter, the basic definition of accounting becomes the basis in discussing the four phases of accounting and introduces the concepts of assets, liabilities, capital, revenue and expenses.

<u>Chapter 3: Analyzing Transactions</u> is about the very first step in the accounting cycle - analysis. The concept of transaction is first discussed here by focusing on the fundamental concepts of value received and given. In the latter part of the chapter, account titles are introduced to be used in the analysis of transactions.

Chapter 4: Journalizing Transactions connects the immediately preceding chapter to the first phase of accounting and considered the second step in the accounting cycle. In this chapter, the concept of T-account is discussed and how it frames the recording process of transactions in the book of original entry called journal. A sample problem is discussed to apply concepts of journalizing by presenting transactions and then illustrating how this is recorded in the journal. Finally, the end part of the chapter differentiates simple from compound entries through examples.

An annex to Chapter 4 is also added after the exercises. The annex talks about how business forms are used to capture business transactions. Examples of journal entries for each type of business form presented are also given to illustrate how business forms become the basis of the journalizing process.

The succeeding Chapter 5: Classifying Transactions Through the Ledger discusses the importance of the book of final entry, the ledger in the consolidation of transactions. In this chapter, the posting of transactions from the journal to the ledger is discussed. A sample posting exercise, based on the previous chapter's illustrative problem, is presented at the end of the chapter.

Chapter 6: Preparing Financial Statements expounds on the third phase of accounting which is the preparation of the financial statements. The chapter opens with the discussion of the trial balance, the initial step in the preparation of financial statements. The preparation of three of the four common basic financial statements is discussed in this chapter – the income statement, statement of changes in equity, and statement of cash flows.

To complete the phases of accounting discussed in the second chapter of the book, Chapter 7: Analyzing Financial Statements presents the three most common financial analysis tools to help users of financial information better understand and appreciate the accounts and amounts contained in the financial statements. The financial statement analysis tools discussed in this chapter are horizontal analysis, vertical analysis, and ratio analysis. Sample problems are also presented to complement the theoretical discussion.

Chapter 8: Accounting for Tourism-related Establishments is a chapter added specifically to emphasize accounting process for an industry. Based on experience, majority of Accounting 1.n students who take up the subject are from tourism or hospitality management courses in the university. As such, this chapter is added to suit the information needs of this group of students, though this can also be interesting to those who would like to read financial statements produced by the hospitality industry.

At the end of the book, a bibliography is presented to encourage readers and users of this book to consult other textbooks or learning materials which may enhance their knowledge regarding the concepts discussed in this material.

It is hoped that this book will become a valuable source for those who would like to learn accounting and appreciate its value in ensuring sustainable and profitable businesses.

> **Additional Notes to Instructor:**
>
> *This book complies with the syllabus for Accounting 1.n. As such the progression of the discussions as well as the level of difficulty in the topics and exercises considers the desired learning outcomes for the course as contained in the syllabus. It also considers, to a great extent, the learning ability of students.*
>
> *Comments, suggestions, as well as requests for solutions manual can be made by sending an email to mikocanares@boholanalysis.com*

This revised edition contains additional exercises at the end of its chapter. A few additional paragraphs were also added in order to ensure that the contents of the book become relevant to current times.

Chapter 1. Businesses and the Need for Financial Information

At the end of the chapter, the student should be able to:

   a. Know and understand the reason why businesses exist.
   b. Classify businesses according to products/services offered.
   c. Identify the common forms of business organization.
   d. Identify the advantages and disadvantages of the different types of business organization.
   e. Understand the need for financial information.
   f. Appreciate the usefulness of financial information.

Why Do Businesses Exist?

Businesses exist for the satisfaction of human needs and wants (Beg and Dash 2010). People who engage in business see a particular human need or want to satisfy or a demand for goods and services that needs to be responded to. For example, in a community where there is no safe drinking water, entrepreneurs may see the problem as an opportunity to establish a water purifying business in order to provide people with clean and safe potable drinking water.

But entrepreneurs do not just engage in business to respond to human needs and wants, but also to earn income (Case et al 2017). This essentially segregates public institutions from private institutions. While public institutions like governments establish service delivery mechanisms like municipal water districts to respond to the need for potable drinking water for public interest, businesses do the same but not for purely public ends but essentially for private gain (Cox 2006). Businesses are established for the purpose of earning profit.

In terms of the types of products that businesses offer, we may be able to classify these into three broad classifications as indicated in Table 1 on the next page:

Classification	*Characteristic*	*Examples*
Manufacturing-concern	Conversion of raw materials into finished products	Manufacturers for soap (Unilever), toothpaste (Colgate-Palmolive), milk (Nestle)
Trading-concern	Selling of manufactured goods to industrial or household consumers	Wholesalers (Fast Cargo Logistics), Supermarkets (SM), Small retailers (sari-sari stores)
Service-concern	Offering of services to the public that otherwise would	Grooming (David's Salon), accommodation (Shangri-La Hotel),

Classification	Characteristic	Examples
	have been provided individually	savings and credit (Union Bank), restaurants (Pizza Hut), transport (Cebu Pacific)

Table 1. Three Major Classification of Businesses According to Products/Services Offered

As indicated above, the classification of businesses describes the type of activities that a particular business offers. For example, manufacturing businesses, or manufacturers, concern themselves with the conversion of raw materials to finished products. Some manufacturing businesses engage in the production of industrial goods (Horngren et al 2015), goods that are used by other manufacturing companies while others engage in the production of consumer goods, or goods that are generally consumed by households (Lopez 2008). An example of an industrial good is limestone, produced by a mining company in Garcia-Hernandez, the Bohol Limestone Corporation for the use of manufacturing companies. On the other hand, Coca-Cola produces Coke, Sprite or Royal Tru-Orange, consumer goods that are used by households and individuals.

Trading-concern businesses are the links between manufacturers and consumers. They facilitate the flow of goods from the manufacturers to the end-users. In this case, there are trading-concern businesses (or traders or merchandisers) that sell to individual consumers, the final or end users. These are those we call as retailers. A classic example of a retailer is your neighbourhood sari-sari store. There are others, however, who sell not to immediate or end-users of products but to retailers. These are what we call as wholesalers. They normally sell in bulk or in massive quantities as compared to retailers. Alturas Supermarket Corporation, for example, a trading corporation based in Tagbilaran City, Bohol, has its mobile wholesaler van that goes to municipalities and sells to retailers.

Finally, service-concern businesses are those that offer services to the public that are otherwise provided individually (Cabrera et al 2010). For example, a mother may cut a child's hair, a son may build his house, or a househelp may cook for the family's dinner. But service provision for these may be done by businesses. The child can go to a barber or beauty shop, the son may contact an engineering and architectural firm, or the family may go to a restaurant for dinner. There are as many service-concern businesses as one can imagine, catering to particular service needs of consumers. There are money-remittance agents (e.g. Western Union), insurance companies (e.g. Pru-life UK), funeral homes (e.g. St. Peter), fast craft service (e.g. Oceanjet), communication providers (e.g. Smart), laundry services (e.g. Perpax), recreation (e.g. ICM Screenville Cinema), among others.

As such, businesses indeed make our lives convenient. They facilitate the satisfaction of our needs and wants. One cannot imagine convenient living without having some, if not all of the businesses mentioned above. Without businesses, we may have to make our own soap and design our toothbrush or paddle our own boat to go to a nearby island.

Businesses also achieve certain public ends like provision of jobs or providing opportunities for farmer-producers to engage in the market (Brue et al 2013). Hotels and resorts for example, are not only major employers, but they are also consumers of the products of farmers and fisherman. Businesses also engage in community services, or what we refer to recently as Corporate Social Responsibility. First Consolidated Bank has a foundation, the FCB Foundation that gives alternative credit source to micro-entrepreneurs while Ford Foundation gives out scholarships to the poor but deserving students.

Nevertheless, while businesses achieve these other ends, it is an undisputed fact that businessmen engage in these enterprises to earn profit.

How are Businesses Organized?

There are at least four most common ways by which businesses are organized in the Philippines. Individuals, for example, establish, operate and manage their own business. Some businesses however, are owned by at least two persons while others are owned by many people. Business organization (or form of ownership) usually falls in one of the following categories:

Business Organization	*Explanation*
Single-proprietorship	A business owned by one person
Partnership	A business owned by two or more persons who "contribute money, property or industry to a common fund with the intention of dividing the profits among themselves".
Corporation	An "artificial being created by operation of law, having the rights of succession, and the powers and attributes provided for by law or by incident to its existence."
Cooperative	An "autonomous and duly registered association of persons, with a common bond of interest, who have voluntarily joined together to achieve their social, economic and cultural needs and aspirations by making equitable contributions to the capital required, patronizing their products and services and accepting a fair share of the risks and benefits of the undertaking in accordance with universally accepted cooperative principles."

Table 2. Common Forms of Business Organization

Sole-proprietorships or single-proprietorships are businesses owned by only one person (Gitman & Zutter 2012). In most cases, small and micro-enterprises are single proprietorships. The reason is obvious. Small and micro-enterprises require a relatively small amount of capital and with simple business processes and systems that fund sourcing and management is manageable at the individual level. Internet café, bakery, automotive machine shop, convenience stores, restaurants, for example are usually sole proprietorships.

But as the demands for capitalization as well as expertise increases, sole-proprietorships are rarely the option for businessmen. They either establish partnerships or corporations. Partnerships and corporations are more complicated to establish than sole proprietorships as they require registration with the Securities and Exchange Commission. Partnerships are less formal than corporations and are smaller and simpler in terms of scope and business operations. Corporations, on the other hand, are more or less permanent ownerships structures with rights of succession (meaning, corporations can continue to exist even when shareholders die or opt out) and legal rights (for example, corporations can acquire property under its name) (De Leon 2013). Normally, large businesses requiring huge amount of capitalization are organized as corporations because fund sourcing is easier through the issuance of capital stock.

In recent years, cooperatives are organized by people who would like to engage in enterprises that would mutually benefit themselves. Cooperativism as a practice begun in Europe and the concept was transported to the Philippine setting, especially with farmers, fishermen, and micro-entrepreneurs. Today, cooperatives are playing a significant role in the local economy in different business activities as power distribution (e.g. electric cooperatives), financing (e.g. cooperative rural banks), production (e.g. Guiwanon Multipurpose Cooperative that produce bottled sardines), and even in the tourism services.

The owner of a sole-proprietorship is referred to as proprietor. Partners are the ones who own partnership. Corporation is owned by shareholders while cooperatives are owned by members. A brief elaboration of the advantages of each form of business is presented in the table below.

	Sole-Proprietorship	Partnership	Corporation	Cooperative
Advantages	• Easy to form • Requires less cost in organization • Benefits accrue to proprietor directly • Proprietor has freedom and flexibility to make	• Easy to form • Requires less cost in organization • Benefits accrue to partners directly • Pools together financial, technical, and	• Continuity in existence • Greater flexibility in raising substantial amounts of capital • Has legal capacity to act in itself	• Continuity in existence • Has flexibility in raising capital • Has legal capacity to act in itself • Members have limited liability • Internal transactions are exempt from

	Sole-Proprietorship	Partnership	Corporation	Cooperative
	decisions	industrial skills of partners	• Shareholders have limited liability	taxation
Disadvantages	• Easily dissolved • Unlimited liability of sole proprietor • Lesser capacity to raise funds • Financial, technical, and industrial skills are limited	• Easily dissolved • Unlimited liability of partners • Lesser capacity to raise funds • Mutual agency of partners may lead to conflicting interest	• Complicated to form and manage • Subject to heavier taxation • Costly to organize and form • Greater degree of government control and intervention	• Collective action problems may exist hampering business operations • Greater degree of government control and intervention • Complicated to organize

Table 3. Advantages and Disadvantages of Different Types of Business Organization

The Need for Financial Information

Whatever be the nature of the business and however it is organized, businesses have one ultimate objective which is to earn profit. Profit is a result when a business' revenues from the sale of its products and services are more than the costs associated with producing and selling the product or providing the service. For example, when a store sells pencils at Php 40 each and the cost of producing and selling one is P30, the store earns a profit of P10 for every pencil it is able to sell.

But this may not always be the case. Businesses too may incur losses. This happens when the costs of operating the business is more than the revenues it received from selling a product or providing the service. In certain situations, revenues equal the costs of producing the product or service. This is what we call a break-even situation. Thus, we can say that there are three possible results when businesses operate – profit, loss, or break-even, as illustrated below:

	Profit	Loss	Break-even
Revenues	P 75,000.00	P 40,000.00	P 50,000.00
Less: Costs and Expenses	50,000.00	50,000.00	50,000.00
Income/(Loss)	25,000.00	(10,000.00)	0.00

Table 4 Three Possible Results of Businesses

How will the owners of the business know whether the business earns or not?

It is important that the business accumulates financial information regularly (Davis et al. 2009). By this we mean that at least the business should record its revenues and expenses. This is financial information at its simplest form. A sari-sari store, for example, (or a convenience store, if you like) will be able to know if it is earning income for a day by just simply listing down all the revenues it receives in terms of sales, and all the expenses pays. It will be able to know what particular products are most sellable or the biggest expense item for the business in a day.

Financial information is important not only for determining profit but also for managing the business (Ainsworth and Deines 2016). Managing the business has four distinct functions – planning, organizing, leading, and controlling (Daft 2015). In these management functions, financial information is a very important component. The value of financial information in each function of the management process is indicated below:

a. Planning – Financial information is necessary in business planning. Knowing how much resources are needed to start the business is a crucial step in determining the viability of the business venture. Even knowing how much money is left at the end of the day to purchase the following day's needs is important. Budgeting, the processes of determining how much and where to get resources and how these resources are to be spent, is an essential component of the management planning exercise.
b. Organizing – How to organize the enterprise, how many people needs to be involved, what are the kinds of expertise needed is also affected by financial information. Even the decision as to what type of organization, be it sole proprietorship, partnership, or corporation to establish to run the business considers financial information. As earlier mentioned, businesses requiring large amounts of capital may be organized as a corporation.
c. Leading – Leading an organization requires a sufficient amount of knowledge in analysing financial information. Direction setting, decision-making processes, and identifying appropriate strategies require sufficient consideration of financial information. For example, deciding to embark on a major advertising campaign requires financial information on whether funds are available or the benefits of doing it would outweigh the costs.
d. Controlling – Ensuring the efficient and effective use of organization's resources is an essential part of management function. Budgets, for example, serve not only as a means to plan for business activities but also to monitor actual figures against budgets. For example, in the case of expenses, budgets will inform managers that the business already spent more than what is allocated for travel and transportation and may need to strategize ways on how to minimize this expense in the future.

Thus, financial information is vital in business operations. Successful business management can never happen without adequate financial information. In like manner, successful managers are those who have the sufficient financial literacy – the ability to read and understand financial data, and make meaningful decisions based on it.

End of Chapter Activities

Exercise 1.1

Name:	Course &year:	Date:
Subject:	Time:	Score:

Discussion Questions:

1. Why is financial information important in business?

2. Give concrete examples in how financial information will affect the four distinct functions of management.

3. What is the best form of business ownership? Why?

4. In your opinion, what are the key characteristics of a manufacturing enterprise?

5. What are the ways that you think businesses can do in order to ensure profitable operations?

6. What must businesses do so that it will know the results of its operation or its financial condition?

Exercise 1.2

Name:	Course &year:	Date:
Subject:	Time:	Score:

Multiple Choice: Select the best answer in each of the following items. Encircle the letter of the answer that corresponds to your choice.

1. Businesses are classified into service-concern, trading, or manufacturing. A restaurant is what type of business?
   - a. trading
   - b. manufacturing
   - c. service-concern
   - d. hybrid
2. Comparing actual amounts spent for particular expenses with what has been budgeted is an example of what function of management?
   - a. planning
   - b. leading
   - c. controlling
   - d. organizing
3. If a business earns more than what it spends, this will result to a
   - a. loss
   - b. profit
   - c. break-even
   - d. none of these
4. The owners of the corporation are referred to as
   - a. sole proprietor
   - b. members
   - c. partners
   - d. shareholders
5. Financial information is not necessary in
   - a. deciding whether to open a new branch or not
   - b. in hiring and firing employees
   - c. in developing a new product or service
   - d. none of these
6. If the objective of businesses is to earn profit, it should make sure that it can
   - a. Maximize its revenues and minimize expenses
   - b. Minimize its revenues and maximize its expenses
   - c. Maximize both revenues and expenses
   - d. None of these
7. Which of the following is not a product of a manufacturing-concern business?
   - a. corned beef
   - b. basket
   - c. peanut kisses
   - d. river cruise
8. Which of the following statements is false?
   - a. If revenues are constant and expenses decrease, profit will increase.
   - b. If revenues decrease and expenses increase, profit will decrease.
   - c. If both revenues and expenses increase, profit will also increase.
   - d. None of these
9. Which of the following business forms is easiest to form and dissolve?
   - a. partnership
   - c. cooperative

      b. single-proprietorship   d. corporation

10. Making budgets at the beginning of the year or at the start of operations is a financial function in

      a. planning   c. organizing
      b. controlling   d. Leading

11. A husband and wife opened a hotel. The business was registered in the name of the wife who manages the day-to-day affairs of the business. The business can be classified as

      a. corporation   c. Partnership
      b. sole-proprietorship   d. None of these

12. Which of the following is not considered an owner of a business?

      a. member   c. Manager
      b. stockholder   d. Partner

13.   Statement 1: When revenue increases but expense remains constant, income increases.

Statement 2: When revenue increases and expense decreases, income increases.

      a.   Both statements are true
      b.   Only statement 1 is true
      c.   Only statement 2 is true
      d.   Both statements are false

14. Examine the following choices. Which do you think is erroneous?

      a. Coca-Cola, Shangri-La, Purefoods, San Miguel
      b. Levis, Penshoppe, Bench, Mossimo
      c. Chowking, Dunkin Donuts, Jollibee, Holiday Taxi
      d. SM, Robinsons, sari-sari store, National Bookstore

15. Financial information is necessary because of the following reasons except

      a. it provides a basis for decision-making
      b. it gives managers a chance to review performance
      c. it helps the business satisfy its customers
      d. it gives owners a view of business operations

Exercise 1.3

Name:		Course &year:	Date:
Subject:		Time:	Score:

True or False: Write TRUE if statement is true and FALSE if otherwise. If your answer is FALSE, encircle the word/s that make the statement erroneous.

__________ 1. Service concern business derive revenues from the sale of goods.

__________ 2. Businesses exist to satisfy human needs and wants.

__________ 3. Trading-concern businesses convert raw materials to finished products.

__________ 4. Businesses make lives of people convenient.

__________ 5. The owner of a partnership is called proprietor.

__________ 6. Stockholders are the owners of a corporation.

__________ 7. Cooperatives are similar to corporations.

__________ 8. All forms of business ownerships are governed by laws.

__________ 9. Corporations have more capacity to raise capital than sole-proprietorships.

__________ 10. Partnerships are easier to form compared to sole-proprietorships.

__________ 11. Corporations cannot sue and be sued.

__________ 12. Businesses do not serve public purposes.

__________ 13. The objective of businesses is to earn profit.

__________ 14. Partners have limited liability.

__________ 15. Stockholders have unlimited liability.

__________ 16. Financial information is not needed in business planning.

__________ 17. Financial information is only needed in controlling financial transactions.

__________ 18. Financial information is needed to determine profit.

__________ 19. A business has loss if it is not generating cash.

__________ 20. A business has profit if its revenues are greater than its expenses.

Exercise 1.4

Name:	Course &year:	Date:
Subject:	Time:	Score:

Classification. Write on the blanks provided the letter S if the business indicated is a service-concern, T if the business is a trading-concern, and M if the business is a manufacturing-concern.

_________ 1. Colgate-Palmolive	_________ 11. Bellevue Hotel
_________ 2. Jansport	_________ 12. H&M
_________ 3. David's Salon	_________ 13. 7 Eleven
_________ 4. Robinson's Supermarket	_________ 14. DHL
_________ 5. Etihad Airways	_________ 15. Citi Hardware
_________ 6. San Miguel Corporation	_________ 16. Metrobank
_________ 7. Toyota	_________ 17. Dell
_________ 8. PLDT	_________ 18. Mr. Quickie
_________ 9. Nestle	_________ 19. Unilab
_________ 10. Titay's Sari-sari Store	_________ 20. Abenson

GROUP WORK

The class may be divided into groups of 5 students to work on the following instructions:

a. The group members will need to think of a business that they would like to organize. At the very least, they should be able to identify the product or service that they would like to offer in detail.
b. They will decide on the following aspects:
    - What is the form of organization? Why?
    - How will they classify their business? Trading? Service? Manufacturing?
    - What is their objective in forming such a business.
c. They will answer the question what they will do so that they will be able to know that their business is doing well on a daily, monthly, or yearly basis.
d. The groups will report their work in class.

Chapter 2. The Role of Accounting in Business

At the end of the chapter, the students are expected to:

a. Learn the accounting terminologies that are essential for them to understand the language of business.
b. Identify the phases of accounting.
c. Appreciate the role of accounting in business.
d. Identify the different users of financial information.
e. Know and understand the Basic Financial Statements and their uses.
f. Know and understand the Critical Underlying assumptions used in accounting.

What is Accounting?

As indicated in the previous chapter, financial information has a key role in business operations that there is a need to record financial data. Recording financial data is so important that even the smallest business organization does it. A sari-sari store for example, keeps a list of the things it purchases or the amounts that a customer owes the business. These are the simplest forms of recording. This can be considered accounting at its most basic and simplest form.

What then is accounting?

There are several definitions of accounting. The Financial Reporting Standards Council, for example defines accounting as "a service activity". "Its function is to provide quantitative information, primarily financial in nature, about economic entities, that is intended to be useful in making economic decisions" (Valix and Peralta 2009).

The definition tells us several things.

a. Accounting is a "service activity". This means that accountants, those performing accounting, are providing a service. This service is the recording, accumulation, and reporting of financial information to enable users to make economic decisions.
b. Accounting's key role as a service activity is to provide financial information to users, about economic entities (Lopez 2008). Economic entities may refer to businesses, or they may also refer to business events.
c. Accounting is necessary because it provides information essential for decision-making (Weygandt et al 2015). This is the critical role of accounting. If financial

information provided out of the accounting process is erroneous, it will be misleading to users and users may make the wrong decisions.

A definition which further details the nature of accounting is provided by the Committee on Accounting Technology of the American Institute of Certified Public Accountants:

> *Accounting is the art of recording, classifying, summarizing, in a significant manner, and in terms of money, transactions, and events, which are in part at least of a financial character and interpreting the results thereof (Valix et al 2010).*

From this definition, we can discuss several functions:

Accounting as an art

The musician captures joy, sadness, love, hope, despair through music. The visual artist captures a majestic scene using his brush. The stage actor portrays a character drawn from real life experiences. Art, in a way, is an act of representation, an exercise of immortalizing a temporary reality. This too is done in accounting. Journal entries in accounting records (something we will learn in the next chapters) captures the essence of a business activity or transaction in accounting books.

Transactions as a central function of accounting exercise

Transactions then play a vital role in the accounting exercise. Transactions are the ones that are recorded in books. Transactions are defined as an exchange in values, where one party in the transaction exchanges values with another (Bazley et al 2010). When one buys a ballpoint pen at the bookstore for example, he gives the counter cashier money in exchange of the ballpoint pen.

There are as many transactions in the business as there are event occurring in it; an owner investing resources in the business, payment of taxes and licenses, payment of rent, selling of goods, purchasing of supplies, payment of salaries, among others. It is to be noted, however, that transactions involve financial values. This is what we refer to as "accountable events" (Edmonds et al. 2014). Transactions are considered such when they have an effect on the assets, liabilities, and capital of the business. These three terms we shall learn in the succeeding pages.

Transactions can be internal or external. The payment of salaries is considered internal, while the payment of taxes is external in nature. As such, internal transactions are those that involve the business entity only while external transactions are those that involve the business and other business entities (Bazley et al 2010).

In this case, we identify, measure, and communicate economic information. This means that not all business activities are recorded as we still have to analyze what are those events that are "accountable." This is the process of identification, also considered as the analytical part of accounting (Weygandt et al 2015). When transactions occur, we still have to decide if these are recorded or not.

Also, there are a set of rules to follow in how we measure transactions. For example, if we receive a piece of land by donation, how do we measure the transaction? By how much should we record the land we receive when we did not spend anything for it? There are rules that govern how this transaction is measured. This is what we call the technical component of accounting (Valix and Peralta 2009) because a set of standards govern the way we record transactions.

Finally, we communicate financial information in a way that is useful to users. This means that we just don't accumulate and report financial information without considering how users of financial information will use what we produce. There are several types of reports that we will learn in the succeeding pages that are designed to help users make financial decisions.

The Phases of Accounting

From the definition, we can elaborate on the four phases of accounting:

Phase	What is this?	How is this done?	Where do we do it?
Recording	The first phase of accounting. This is when we record transactions for the first time in accounting books and records.	Through journal entries. A journal entry, we will learn later on, has debit and credit components.	The JOURNAL. Also referred to as the book of original entry.
Classifying	The second phase of accounting. This is when transactions that are already recorded are classified into groups of similar accounts.	Through ledger entries. Journal entries are transferred from the journal to the ledger.	The LEDGER. Also referred to as the book of final entry.
Summarizing	The preparation of financial statements and reports.	Through the preparation of a worksheet which facilitates the preparation of financial statements.	The FINANCIAL STATEMENTS which are quantitative presentations of the results of operations, financial position, cash flows and changes in equity of the business.
Interpreting	The analysis of financial information to aid users in decision-making.	Through different financial analysis tools as vertical analysis, horizontal analysis, and ratio analysis.	Through MANAGEMENT REPORTS accompanying financial statements.

Table 5. Four Phases of Accounting

Money as a unit of Measure

Because we record in accounting transactions, we need to use a particular unit of measure. In recording age of children, we use years. In recording weight of harvested rice, we use kilograms. In recording distance, we use kilometres. In accounting for business transactions, we use money, a unit of currency, as a unit of measure (Jeter and Chaney 2014).

In which case, we record transactions using the Philippine peso. If we have transactions that are denominated in foreign currency, like for example, buying merchandise from the US in US dollars, we record them using the Philippine peso by using foreign exchange conversion rates at the date of payment.

What is the Basic Purpose of Accounting?

The American Accounting Association defines accounting as "the process of identifying, measuring, and communicating economic information to permit informed judgment and decision by users of the information" (Lopez 2008). Based on this definition, we can say that the purpose of accounting is to provide financial information to users that they can make informed judgement and better decision.

Users of financial information

As accounting is a service activity, it provides a particular service, the provision of financial information to users. There are various kinds of users of financial information as indicated below:

a. Owners/investors – they are concerned with financial information that has a particular bearing on their investment. They would like to know if the business is profitable so that they would be able to decide whether to keep or give up their investment by selling it to others.
b. Management – financial information can be made as a basis in determining the effectiveness and efficiency of management. Profits, for example, may indicate the effectiveness of the marketing people in achieving sales targets or the efficiency of the manufacturing department in keeping costs of production to the minimum.
c. Employees – employees are concerned whether or not their employer has the capacity to provide them competitive remuneration, benefits and opportunities.
d. Creditors – banks and financial institutions require businesses to submit financial statements when applying for loan so that they will be able to assess capability to pay obligations. Even suppliers who give credit to businesses need financial information to assess credit-worthiness and set credit limits
e. Government agencies – Governments have regulatory powers over businesses. The Bureau of Internal Revenue, for example, needs financial statements to assess taxes to be collected from businesses. The Securities and Exchange

Commission requires the submission of financial statements from corporations. Even the local government units require financial information from businesses to compute the amount of annual business permits.

These are but just a few of the different users of financial information. There are others still like financial press and reporting agencies, business advisers and analysts, customers, and academic institutions. We can say even that the public has an interest in financial information. It is for this reason that accountants prepare "general-purpose financial statements" (Larson et al 2005) or financial statements that serve the purpose of all types of users.

The Basic Financial Statements

The accounting standards mentions at least six components of financial statements. We will only deal with four basic financial statements in this chapter:

a. Income Statement

This is currently known as the Statement of Financial Operations, or Statement of Comprehensive Income. This practically shows the results of operations of the business for a period of time (Kieso et al 2016). As a statement, it showcases the profit/loss equation which states that

$$\text{Revenues} - \text{Expenses} = \text{Net Income/Net Loss}$$

Where:

Revenues represent the amount received or collectible from the sale of merchandise (e.g. sarisari store), the rendering of services (e.g. barbershop), the use of entity's resources (e.g. buildings for rent) or sale of assets other than products (e.g. sale of used cars). (Ainsworth and Deines 2016)

Expenses represent the necessary disbursements or obligations in operating a business (Kimwell 2007). This may be in the form of cost of sales (e.g. the cost of producing a ballpen), selling expenses (e.g. the salaries of marketing personnel), administrative expenses (e.g. office supplies), other expenses, and income tax expense.

As earlier indicated, when revenues exceed expenses, there is a net income but when expenses exceed revenues, there is a net loss.

b. Balance Sheet

The Balance Sheet, currently known as Statement of Financial Position shows the financial condition of a business as of a given period of time (Hurt 2016). As a statement, it showcases what is referred to as the Basic Accounting Equation, which states that

$$\boxed{\text{Assets} = \text{Liabilities} + \text{Capital}}$$

Where:

Assets are the economic resources of the company from which future benefits are expected to flow to the entity (Cabrera et al 2010). When a business has land, for example, it is an asset because the business may generate cash from it by using it as collateral to a loan or by selling it.

Liabilities are economic obligations of a business which are expected to result to a future outflow of resources (Horngren et al 2015). When a business for example, borrows from a bank, it has the obligation to pay such amount in the future plus interest. In which case, when the business actually pays the liability, it will have to give up some of its resources.

Capital represents the interest of the owners in the business (Weygandt et al 2015). Simply put, it is the amount of resources that the owner puts into the business, including the income or loss charged against it. Capital is also referred to as owner's equity.

The equation above suggests that all assets owned by the business has two main sources – either it is provided by creditors (liability) or the owners (capital). If for example, the business has money amounting to P100,000, and all of these are provided by the owner, the basic accounting equation will look like this:

P100,000   =   0   +   P100,000
(Assets)   (Liabilities)   (Capital)

If P40,000 was borrowed from the bank and the rest invested by the owner, the basic accounting equation will look like this:

P100,000   =   P40,000   +   P60,000
(Assets)   (Liabilities)   (Capital)

c. Statement of Changes in Equity

The Statement of Changes in Equity is a statement that presents the changes in the capital account (Kimwell 2007). In the case of sole-proprietorships (the form of business ownership that we will deal with in this book), there are at least four major events that would affect the capital account, and these are as follows:

- Additional investment – happens when the owner invests more assets to the business. In this case, capital (or equity) increases.
- Withdrawal/Drawing – happens when the owner gets assets from the business for personal use. For example, when the owner will withdraw cash from the business to spend for his own, this will have an effect of decreasing his capital in the business.
- Income from operations – when the business earns net income, capital of the owner will increase.
- Loss from operations – this happens when the expenses of the business exceeds its revenues. Consequently, loss decreases capital.

d. Statement of Cash Flows

The statement of cash flows is a financial statement dedicated to cash. Cash, as an asset, plays a critical function in business because transactions normally start off with cash and ends in it. Thus, the statement of cash flows monitors all the inflows (receipts) and outflows (disbursements) of the business with the intention of computing the cash balance at the end.

The Five Basic Accounting Values

The discussion on income statement and balance sheet above reveals the five basic accounting values. These are assets (economic resources), liabilities (economic obligations), capital (owner's equity), revenue (sales of goods or services) and expenses (disbursements necessary in earning the revenue).

The accounting values were also earlier segregated into two equations – the basic accounting equation and profit and loss. But what is the relationship between the two?

- Revenues increase assets, while expenses decrease it. If there are more revenues than expenses, then there will be a net increase in assets. If there are more expenses than revenues, there will be a net decrease in assets.
- Expenses incurred but not paid increases liabilities. Consequently, there is a future decrease in assets if liabilities have to be paid.
- Net income increases capital while net loss decreases it. For example, a fish trader who uses his own money of P500 (his capital) to buy fish and sell all of it at the end of the day for P800, will earn income of P300. In which case, the amount of capital available for the next day to buy fish is P300 more than when the fish trader started. The capital available for the next day is reduced if there is a loss.

What are the Critical Underlying Assumptions used in Accounting?

The following are the principles that accounting assumes in the preparation of financial statements:

1. Accounting Entity

Simply put, the accounting entity assumption posits that the business is separate and distinct from the owner (Horngren et al 2015). As such, in recording business transactions, we take the perspective of the business in mind, which means to say that we record transactions as if we are the business, and not the owner. This also requires that business assets should be treated separately from the personal assets of the owner.

2. Going Concern

Going concern means that the life of the business is indefinite and thus must be assumed to be continuous (Bazley et al 2010). In this case, expenses not yet paid but are already incurred are recorded in accounting records because it is assumed that the business will still exist the following period to be able to pay it. The same is true for the recording of income already earned but not yet received. The going concern assumption supports this.

3. Time Period

Because the life of the business is indefinite, the evaluation of business is done periodically. Thus, preparation of financial statements, for example, is done as frequent as management wants it to aid them in their decision-making processes.

The basic accounting period is one year (annual). Annual period can either be calendar year or fiscal year. The calendar year starts from January and ends with December while the fiscal year starts with any month of the year and ends on the 12th month thereafter. There are also shorter periods than the annual. These are semi-annual (6 months), monthly (4 weeks), bimonthly (2 weeks). Rarely do businesses prepare financial statements on a daily basis.

4. Accrual

Accrual allows the recording of income even when not yet received as long as these are earned, or the recording of expenses even when not yet disbursed as long as these are incurred (Ainsworth and Deines 2016). This principle allows the proper matching of expenses against revenues. For example, if the business has not yet paid its rent at the end of an accounting period but has actually used the premises, then the business needs to record the rent expense, even when not yet paid. Not doing so would understate expenses for the period, and thus would overstate revenues.

5. Monetary Unit

As earlier mentioned in this chapter, transactions are recorded using a currency as a unit of measure. Thus, in the case of the Philippines, all transactions are recorded in the Philippine peso, even those that are denominated in foreign currency.

End of Chapter Activities:

Exercise 2.1

Name:	Course &year:	Date:
Subject:	Time:	Score:

Discussion Questions:

1. Which among the accounting definitions mentioned in this chapter you think is most appropriate to describe accounting? Why?

2. Why is accounting, as a science and as a discipline, considered critical and important in business management?

3. Why do you think that money, and not other measure, is used to value transactions in recording?

4. Reflect on your current financial position. How much assets do you have? How much liabilities? How will you convert your current financial status into a basic accounting equation?

5. Why is accounting entity an important underlying assumption in accounting?

6. What do you think are the two ways by which a business will be able to increase its net income? Use the profit and loss equation as basis.

7. How often should businesses make financial statements? Why do you think so?

8. What is the relationship between the basic accounting equation and the profit and loss equation?

Exercise 2.2

Name:	Course &year:	Date:
Subject:	Time:	Score:

Multiple Choice. Select the best answer in each of the following items. Encircle the letter that corresponds to your choice.

1. Which of the following is incorrectly stated?
    a. $A = L + C$ b. $A - L = C$ c. $A - C = L$ d. None of these
2. The financial statement that shows the financial position of a given business as of a period of time
    a. Income statements
    b. Business documents
    c. Balance sheet
    d. Business transactions
3. The following are 'accountable' except
    a. Investment of equipment in the business
    b. Withdrawal of cash for personal use
    c. Approval of vacation leave for an employee
    d. Borrowing of additional cash from the bank for expansion purposes.
4. Which of the following statements is not true about the accounting equation?
    a. Income increase capital
    b. Drawing decrease capital
    c. Expenses decrease capital
    d. Asset decrease capital
5. If revenue is P80,000, expenses are P40, 000, and withdrawals are P50,000, the amount of increase(decrease) in capital is
    a. P10,000 increase
    b. P50,000 increase
    c. P10,000 decrease
    d. P50,000 decrease
6. Which of the following statements is incorrect?
    a. Revenue increases capital
    b. Expense decreases assets
    c. Expense decreases capital
    d. Revenue decreases asset
7. If the business had liabilities of P10,000 and owner's equity of P40,000, assets equal
    a. P10,000   b. P50,000   c. P30,000   d. P40,000
8. Which of the following principle requires that financial statements should be prepared periodically to allow users to make decisions responsive to current situations?
    a. going concern
    b. accrual
    c. time period
    d. accounting entity
9. The records of the business must contain transactions that occur in the business only without considering the personal transactions of its owner. This is an illustration of the principle of
    a. going concern
    b. accrual
    c. time period
    d. accounting entity

10. Which of the following users is interested in knowing the financial position of an enterprise so that he would be able to gauge the capacity of his employer to provide him gainful and secure employment?
    a. a stock broker   c. corporate lawyer
    b. financial adviser   d. employee
11. Recognizing an income even when not received so long as it is earned is an application of the principle of
    a. Conservatism   c. accrual
    b. going concern   d. time period
12. Statement 1: Expenses are necessary consequence of generating revenues.
    Statement 2: Withdrawals from the business by the owner decrease capital or
        investment.
    a. both statements are true   c. only statement 1 is true
    b. both statements are false   d. only statement 2 is true
13. Statement 1: Net income increases capital while net loss decreases capital.
    Statement 2: The capital account is increased by revenues and decreased by
        withdrawals and expenses
    a. both statements are true   c. only statement 1 is false
    b. both statements are false   d. only statement 2 is false
14. All transactions need to be valued in a currency unit. This is an expression of what principle?
    a. banking principle   c. monetary unit
    b. currency   d. None of these
15. The financial statement that shows the receipts and disbursements of cash as of a particular period.
    a. Financial position   c. Cash flows
    b. Results of operations   d. Changes in equity
16. The financial statement that shows the profitability performance of a business as of a given time period.
    a. Financial position   c. Cash flows
    b. Results of operations   d. Changes in equity
17. Which is not part of a complete set of basic financial statements?
    a. Accounting policies and notes   c. Financial position
    b. Cash flows   d. None of these
18. Which of the following users will be very interested in profitability information of a particular business?
    a. Bank   c. Government
    b. Investor   d. All of these
19. Which of the following is incorrectly stated?
    a. Total Assets can remain constant even with a happening of a transaction.
    b. Liabilities can increase or decrease assets.
    c. Any increase in asset will always cause an increase in capital.
    d. None of these
20. When revenues are greater than expenses, which of the following is not true?
    a. there is net income   c. assets increase
    b. capital increase   d. None of these

Exercise 2.3

Name:	Course &year:	Date:
Subject:	Time:	Score:

Computations. In each of the given items, compute for the missing (?) figures.

Part 1. Basic Accounting Equation

	Asset	Liability	Capital
1	100,000	40,000	?
2	55,0000	?	20,000
3	?	80,000	40,000
4	68,500	?	22,300
5	79,560	34,480	?

Part 2. Revenue/Expense Equation

	Revenue	Expense	Net Income/(Loss)
1	100,000	62,500	?
2	55,0000	?	(20,000)
3	?	98,520	39,560
4	152,390	?	97,420
5	78,650	128,550	?

Exercise 2.4

Name:	Course &year:	Date:
Subject:	Time:	Score:

Computations. Solve for the required amounts in each of the given problem.

1. Debid's Saloon had many customers on July 2, 2018, a Monday. The total money received by the cashier from customers during that day amounted to P29,640.00. The cashier paid P6,000 of salaries for the service personnel during that day and consumed approximately P2,800 in light and water, as well as supplies. If these are the only expenses for the day, how much net income/loss did Debid's Salon earn?

2. When Whatcha Macallit opened his business for the first time on July 15, 2018, his business assets consisted of tables and chairs amounting to P25,000; equipment with a value of P187,500, and total cash of P10,000. If these assets were funded 40% from debts, how much is Macallit's capital?

3. Bebe, the owner of Mang Kinasal received a total of P125,268 from the cashier of her store. This represents the sales for the day after deducting P32,400 of expenses. How much was the total revenue for the day?

4. Dammy, owner of Damgo Sari Sari Store, would like to sell his whole business to his sister, Dreams on June 31, 2018. As of that date, the total assets of the store amounted to P3,250,650. Dammy, however, has a loan at that bank amounting to P2,000,000 on that day. If you are Dammy and would like to sell to Dreams the store of its net worth, how much would you be willing to receive?

Exercise 2.5

Name:	Course &year:	Date:
Subject:	Time:	Score:

Matching Type. Match column (A) with the correct answer in column (B). Write on the blank before the words in column (A) the letter in column (B) that matches your answer.

	Column A		Column B
_______ 1	Accounting	a	Involves the business only
_______ 2	Transactions	b	Financial statements
_______ 3	Accountable events	c	Assess the ability of the business to pay
_______ 4	Recording	d	Assets = Liabilities + Capital
_______ 5	Unit of measure	e	Service activity
_______ 6	Owners	f	Done using the ledger
_______ 7	Internal	g	Cash receipts and disbursements
_______ 8	Income statement	h	Intangibles
_______ 9	Changes in equity	i	Exchange of values
_______ 10	Cash flows	j	Money
_______ 11	Classifying	k	Investment
_______ 12	Creditors	l	Expense
_______ 13	Summarizing	m	Has effect on accounting values
_______ 14	Balance Sheet	n	Changes in the capital account
_______ 15	External	o	Concerned with their investments
		p	Done in the journal
		q	Revenue-Expenses=Net Income or Loss
		r	Drawing
		s	Involves the business and other partners

GROUP WORK

Go back to the group work you did in the previous chapter. If you will be setting up the business, answer the following questions:

a. What things will you need to buy and put in place before the business starts?
b. What will be the preparatory activities that you will do?
c. Where will you get the money that you will need to set up the business?
d. How much will you invest?
e. Initially compute for"
- Total assets
- Total Liabilities
- Capital

Chapter 3. Analysing Transactions

At the end of the chapter the students should be able to:
  a.   Understand business transactions and how these are to be accounted
  b.   Identify value received and value parted with in analysing business transactions
  c.   Learn the common account titles and understand how they are used in recording business transactions
  d.   Appreciate how the reciprocal nature of transactions affect the accounting process

While the accounting process starts off with journalizing as its first major activity, transactions cannot be journalized if one does not have a clear understanding of the transaction. In this chapter, we will deal with the analysis of transactions as a major step in actually recording the transaction in the journals.

Transaction Defined

We can define a business transaction as an "exchange of values" (Kieso et al 2016). There are certain implicit assumptions in this definition.

First, transactions happen between two parties. The parties may be internal to the organization, like the corporation paying the salaries of its workers. The parties may also consist of one from within the organization and another external to it, as in the case of a business buying goods from a supplier.

Secondly, transactions happen when there is an exchange. This means to say that each party to the transaction gives, and consequently receives something. For example, when one buys bread, he gives money to the sales lady at the bread counter and brings home the bread in exchange. The saleslady, in like manner, receives the money before handing out the bread to the customer.

Thirdly, the things exchanged carries financial value. For example, when one goes to the barbershop to have a haircut, the services that the barber gives carries financial value, and is never at all free. In like manner, the money that the customer gives to the barber is of course valuable in itself.

Finally, the values exchanged are assumed to be equal. In which case, what one receives is assumed to be of the same value as what one gives. Thus, in the examples given above, the bread is of the same value as what the customer paid for it, and the barber's services is of the same value as the money that the customer gives him.

Transactions and Accountable Events

There are many events in the life of a business, but not all of them can be considered business transactions. There are many events in the life of the business but not all of them can be considered "accountable". An accountable event, therefore, is one which can be recorded in the books of accounts and these are those which have an effect on a business' assets, liabilities, and capital (Horngren et al 2015).

For example, the opening of the business, complete with ribbon cutting and the presence of important guests is an event, but it is not necessarily a business transaction. It is also an event, but it is not necessarily accountable. Thus, not all events are transactions that can be recorded in the books of accounts.

But the cash purchase of office supplies, for example, is an accounting event which can also be considered a business transaction, and also an accountable event. In this transaction, the buyer gives out cash in exchange for office supplies. Correspondingly, it has an effect to one basic accounting value – assets. Assets increase and decrease at the same time. Cash is an asset, and it decreased because it was used to pay the purchase. Office supplies, another asset, increased because it was received after the payment.

It must be noted, that when we identify the values received and given in every transaction, we assume the position of the business. As such, when we analyze transactions, we are the business, and not the owner. Therefore, in the transaction above, it is the business that purchased the supplies, and correspondingly paid in cash. It is important to remember this because it will have tremendous effect on how we deal with owner-business transactions later on.

Identifying Values Received and Parted With

It is important then to be able to know what the values are received and given in a transaction. Below, we present the values received and given for a set of transactions. This is presented to aid you in understanding the succeeding discussions:

Transaction	Value Received	Value Parted With
1. Bought equipment for cash	Equipment	Cash
2. Received cash for services rendered	Cash	Service
3. Paid for electric bill	Electricity	Cash

In transaction 1 above, the business bought equipment and paid in cash. Clearly, what the business will receive is equipment, and what it gives up is cash. In transaction

2, we rendered services and we correspondingly received cash. In transaction 3, we paid for electric bill, and thus we received electricity service and gave out cash.

However, to facilitate things easier, it may be necessary to use account titles than common or ordinary-usage words to describe what is received and what is given. Account titles are words or phrases used in accounting to capture a financial value. In which case, account titles are the ones we use to record transactions in business.

Account Titles

We present below the common account titles used in businesses, more particularly for sole proprietorships offering services to consumers. The account titles are classified based on the five accounting values earlier discussed. The five accounting values are assets, liabilities, capital, revenue, and expense.

The shaded rows represent major classifications of a particular accounting value. Assets, for example, are classified as current or non-current.

Assets:

Account Title	Description
Current Assets	*(Assets readily convertible to cash)*
Cash on Hand	Cash not deposited in banks and are kept within business premises
Cash in bank	Cash deposited in bank. This may take the form of a savings account, a current account (or checking account), or a time deposit
Accounts Receivable	Amounts collectible from customers as a result of a past sales transaction
Supplies Inventory	Unused supplies on hand. This may be office supplies (e.g. bond paper, pens, staple wire, etc), store supplies (e.g. packing cellophanes, binding straw, etc.), shop supplies (e.g. lubricants, in the case of a machine shop).
Notes Receivable	Amounts collectible from customers as a result of a past sales transaction, but supported by promissory notes
Non-current Assets	*(Assets not readily convertible to cash)*
Land	Land owned and used by the business
Building	Building owned and used by the business
Equipment	Equipments needed for offering the service to customers. This may be shop equipment (e.g. an oven for a bakeshop), a delivery equipment (e.g. a multicab delivering water for a water refilling station), a transportation equipment (e.g. bus for a transport company), or store equipment (e.g. a cash register in a supermarket).
Furniture and Fixtures	Tables, chairs, display shelves, cabinets, lockers, benches, sala set, among others of the same nature
Machinery	Machines needed for business operations. An example would be a welding machine in an auto repair shop.

Liabilities:

Account Title	Description
Current Liabilities	*(Obligations payable within one year or the normal operating cycle whichever is shorter))*
Accounts Payable	Obligations to pay for the purchase of goods or services.
Notes Payable	These are obligations that are supported by a promissory note
Non-Current Liabilities	*(Obligations payable normally beyond one year)*
Loans Payable	Obligations to pay for money borrowed from banks and financial institutions
Mortgage Payable	Obligations to pay for borrowed money with property of the business as collateral. When land or any immovable property is used as collateral, this is referred to as real estate mortgage. If movable property like car is used as collateral, this is referred to as chattel mortgage.

Capital:

Account Title	Description
Owners' Capital	Owner's investment in the business which may include cash, property or other assets
Owner's Drawing	Withdrawal of owners from the business

Revenue:

Account Title	Description
Service Income	Receipt from customers for services rendered. This may be in the form of professional fees (professional fees income), service fees (dental, medical, etc), or other forms of service income (e.g. barber shops, vulcanizing shops)
Other Income	Miscellaneous income apart from the major source of income
Interest Income	Income from loans receivable, or from bank deposits

Expenses

Account Title	Description
Salaries and Wages	Payment to workers for services rendered
Rent Expense	Payment to the owner of leased premises
Supplies Expense	Supplies used by the business
Light and Water Expense	Payment for electricity and water bills
Communications Expense	Payment to telephone/cellular phone companies, and for postage and handling of letters,
Taxes and License	Payment of business permits, revenue taxes, and other related fees

Account Title	Description
Insurance Expense	Payment of premium for company insurances

The list as contained above is not comprehensive. These are just a few of the examples that we would like to present for use in the identification of value received and value parted with.

Using Account Titles

In the example below, we present transactions and we use the account titles we presented in determining value received and value parted with.

Transaction	Value Received	Value Parted With
1. Bought equipment for cash	Equipment	Cash
2. Received cash for services rendered	Cash	Service Income
3. Paid for electric bill	Light and Water	Cash
4. Paid salaries of employees	Salaries and Wages	Cash
5. Rendered services and received a promissory note	Notes Receivable	Service Income
6. The owner withdrew cash for personal use	Owner's Drawing	Cash
7. The owner invested machinery in the business	Machinery	Owner's Capital
8. Borrowed money from the bank	Cash	Loans Payable
9. Paid rent for office building	Rent Expense	Cash
10. Collected in full the account of a customer	Cash	Accounts Receivable

As indicated in the examples above, we now use account titles to determine the value received and the value parted with. More examples of this exercise are given at the end of the chapter.

End of Chapter Activities

Exercise 3.1

Name:	Course &year:	Date:
Subject:	Time:	Score:

Discussion Questions. Individually or in groups, reflect on the following questions below:

a. Will there be instances that we receive things of value, but we do not give anything in return? What are these instances? How do you think should we deal with this in accounting?

b. Accounting is said to be the language of business. Given your learnings from this chapter, what do you think is the reason why this is so?

c. What is the difference between accountable and non-accountable events? When do we say that events are accountable? When do we say that they are not?

Exercise 3.2

Name:	Course &year:	Date:
Subject:	Time:	Score:

Matching Type. *Write on the blank after each question the letter of the answer that corresponds to your choice*

<u>Choices:</u>

a) Accounts Receivable	n) Depreciation
b) Owner's equity	p) Prepaid Rent
c) Taxes and Licenses Payable	q) Withdrawal
d) Utilities payable	r) account names
e) Cash on hand	s) Office Supplies
f) Accounting equation	t) Rights
g) Land	u) Salary Expenses
h) Advertising Expense	v) Assets
i) Capital	w) chattel
j) Freight-in	
k) Notes receivable	
l) Professional fees	
m) SSS Payable	

<u>Questions:</u>

1. Coins and bills in the possession of the business ______
2. Rights of the owner in the business ______
3. flyers, radio announcements, etc. ______
4. Properties of the business, tangible or intangible ______
5. Amount paid for service of employees ______
6. Income derived in the practice of profession ______
7. Mortgage with car as collateral ______
8. Collectible from clients for services rendered on account ______
9. Obligations owed for the use of electricity ______
10. Amount due to government ______
11. Amount collectible from clients and supported with
      promissory notes ______
12. Bond paper, ball pens, paperclips ______
13. Payable to SSS ______
14. A=L+C ______
15. Decrease in investment ______

Exercise 3.3

Name:	Course &year:	Date:
Subject:	Time:	Score:

Identification. Give the account title in each of the following items. Write your answer on the blank provided after each item.

1. Coins and bills in the possession of the business
   ____

2. Owner's investment in the business
   ____

3. Payment of the owner for occupied building
   ____

4. Chairs, tables, cabinets, among others
   ____

5. Issued promissory note for merchandise purchased
   ____

6. Amount paid for services of employees
   ____

7. Income derived in the practice of profession
   ____

8. Computers, typewriters, fax machine, etc.
   ____

9. Payable to suppliers for bought supplies
   ____

10. Loan with the bank
   ____

11. Collectible from clients for services rendered on account
   ____

12. Payment of electricity and water bills
   ____

13. Amount due to government in the form of business permits
   ____

14. Amount collectible from clients and supported with promissory notes
   ____

15. Income from deposits in the bank
   ____

16. Plastic bags, tapes, stapler fillers, etc. used in the store
   ____

17. Costs incurred to promote the products of the business
   ____

18. Delivery truck

____

19. Expense already incurred but not yet paid

____

20. Revenues of a barber shop

____

Exercise 3.4

Name:	Course &year:	Date:
Subject:	Time:	Score:

Identifying Value Received and Value Parted With. Indicate the value received and the value parted with using the following transactions. Write your answer on the space provided. A sample is provided at the beginning.

	Value Received	Value Given
Example: The owner made an initial cash investment in the business.	*Cash*	*Owner's Capital*
1. Received amount borrowed from bank		
2. Additional investment in the business		
3. Cash withdrawal for personal use		
4. Bought delivery truck on account and issued a promissory note		
5. Bought machinery for cash		
6. Received cash from customers on account		
7. Received cash from cash customers		
8. Paid amount due to the bank		
9. Acquired delivery truck for cash		
10. Paid taxes and licenses		

Exercise 3.5

Name:	Course &year:	Date:
Subject:	Time:	Score:

Identification. Classify the following items. On the space provided, write A if assets, L if liabilities, C if capital, R if revenue, and E if expense.

1. Professional Fees   _____
2. Unused Supplies   _____
3. Interest Receivable   _____
4. Service Income   _____
5. Rent Revenue   _____
6. Cash on hand   _____
7. Interest Income   _____
8. Salaries and Wages   _____
9. Loans Payable   _____
10. Owner's Capital   _____

11. Interest Payable   _____
12. Prepayments   _____
13. Accounts Payable   _____
14. Mortgage Payable   _____
15. Accounts Receivable   _____
16. Taxes and Licenses   _____
17. S, Drawing   _____
18. Cash in Bank   _____
19. Supplies Expense   _____
20. Office Equipment   _____

Exercise 3.6

Name:	Course &year:	Date:
Subject:	Time:	Score:

Transaction Analysis. Indicate the value received and value parted with in each of the following transactions:

Mr. Balikbayan opened a plumbing service called Balik Works. The following business transactions were completed for the month of October.

Oct	1	Balikbayan invested cash of P20,000 in the business
	5	Purchased supplies worth P500.00 and paid cash
	7	Rendered plumbing services to customers on account, P750.00
	10	Bought additional equipment on account, P3,000.00
	15	Paid P9,000.00 for office furniture
	16	Collected P4000.00 from customers on account
	18	Received cash of P10,000.00 from various customers
	20	Paid 50% of account on October 10
	25	Made a cash withdrawal of P400.00
	30	Additional investment, P1,000.00
	31	Paid salaries of workers, P5,000

The following account titles should be used.

Cash	Accounts Payable
Accounts Receivable	Balikbayan, Capital
Supplies	Balikbayan, Withdrawal
Equipment	Service Income
Office Furniture	Salaries Expense

Use the table below in answering the exercise:

Date	Value Received	Value Parted With
Oct 1		
Oct 5		
Oct 7		
Oct 10		
Oct 15		

Date	Value Received	Value Parted With
Oct 16		
Oct 18		
Oct 20		
Oct 25		
Oct 30		
Oct 31		

Exercise 3.7

Name:	Course &year:	Date:
Subject:	Time:	Score:

Transaction Analysis. Indicate the value received and value parted with in each of the following transactions:

Ms. ChrisJul owns a self-service laundry shop. She started the business in January and the following business transactions occurred during the month. The laundry shop operates on a cash basis.

Jan	1	ChrisJul invested the following:

<pre>
Jan   1   ChrisJul invested the following:
                  Washing Machine + Dryer   P450,000
                  Detergent and Fabric Softener   20,000
                  Tables and Chairs   80,000
                  Money   50,000
      2   Received P3,200 from various customers for laundry services
      3   Received P2,900 from various customers for laundry services
      5   Received P1,800 from various customers for laundry services
      7   Paid 2,400 salaries of workers for the week
      8   Bought additional dryer on account for P40,000
      12   Received cash of P3,200.00 from various customers
      14   Paid 60% of account on January 8
      18   Received cash from various customers for services
      22   ChrisJul withdrew P5,000 cash from the business
      24   Paid light and water bill, P4,600
      30   Paid salaries of workers for 3 weeks P8,600
</pre>

The following account titles should be used.

Cash	Accounts Payable
Laundry Supplies	ChrisJul, Capital
Laundry Equipment	ChrisJul, Withdrawal
Shop Furniture	Service Income
Office Furniture	Light and Water
	Salaries Expense

Use the table below in answering the exercise:

Date	Value Received	Value Parted With
Jan 1		
Jan 2		

Date	Value Received	Value Parted With
Jan 3		
Jan 5		
Jan 7		
Jan 8		
Jan 12		
Jan 14		
Jan 18		
Jan 22		
Jan 24		
Jan 30		

GROUP WORK

Using the business that you envisioned at the beginning of this book, prepare the following requirements below:

a. Imagine the transactions that could possibly happen to your business in a week or month. Write them down. To be more specific, assign peso values to your transactions and dates.
b. Construct a table in the same manner as the exercise above.
c. Analyse the value received and value parted for each of the transaction identified. Use the table you constructed for this purpose.

Chapter 4. Journalizing Transactions

At the end of the chapter the students are expected to:
  a. Understand the proper use of general journals.
  b. Learn the proper use of T-accounts.
  c. Know the procedures in recording transactions in the journal.
  d. Enter transactions into journal sheets

As indicate in Chapter 1 of this book, accounting is a process towards a particular objective, which is the preparation of financial statements that reflect the results of operations, financial condition, and cash flows of a particular entity as of or within a given period of time. As a process, it consists of a series of steps to attain this objective. Very briefly, the diagram below shows the progression of these steps, in their proper order:

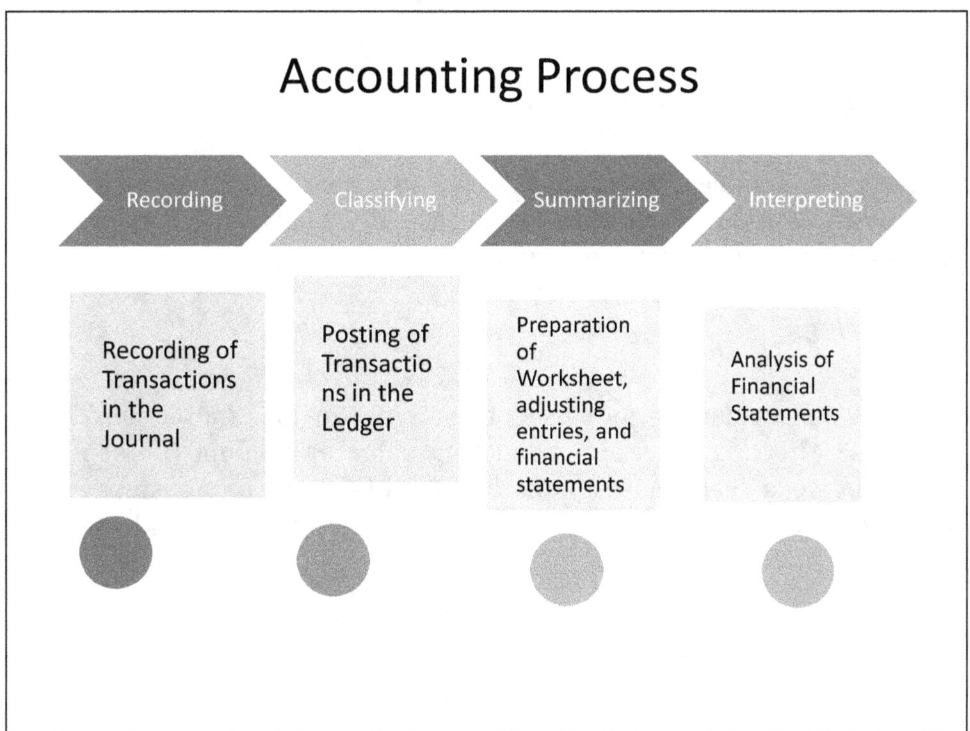

As indicated in the diagram above, accounting is composed of at least four phases. The recording phase involves recording the transactions in the journal, hence the term journalizing. The subsequent phase, classifying, involves posting the recorded transactions in the ledger. The summarizing phase involves the preparation of worksheet, the recording of adjusting entries and the drafting of financial statements. Finally, the interpreting phase involves the analysis of financial statements to allow a more meaningful reading of prepared financial statements. The focus of this chapter is on journalizing, the first step in the accounting process.

How do we record transactions?

Needless to say, we need to analyze transactions first before we will be able to record it because we need to know first what is to be debited, and what is to be credited. A straightforward way of doing it is to go back to the skills you developed in the previous chapter – by knowing what value is given and value received. Value received is always the debit part of the journal entry. Value parted with or value given is always the credit side of part of the journal entry. This is illustrated below:

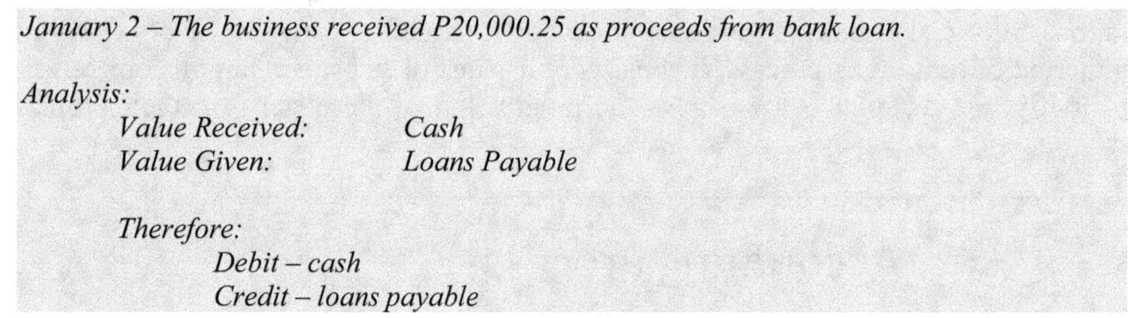

January 2 – The business received P20,000.25 as proceeds from bank loan.

Analysis:
>   *Value Received:*   *Cash*
>   *Value Given:*   *Loans Payable*

>   *Therefore:*
>   *Debit – cash*
>   *Credit – loans payable*

However, there are complex transactions that may not be analysed on value received and value parted with only, and therefore needs to be analyzed on the basis of accounting values. In this case we use what we refer to as a T –account.

T-Account and Its Uses

A T-Account is an accounting tool used to summarize the transactions for a particular period of time affecting a certain accounting value or account (Larson et al 2005, 53-54). In which case, a T-account is prepared for all accounts of a business. The T- Account, however, is composed of 2 sides – the debit side, and the credit side and this is illustrated below:

Account

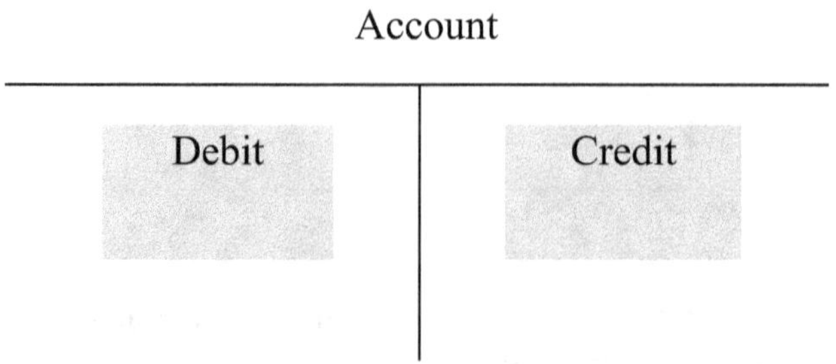

The left side of the account is the debit side while the right side is the credit side. Each account, therefore, has a debit and a credit side. Also, each account has a normal balance side (be it debit or credit), and this is the side of the T-account where that particular account will increase its balance. The opposite side of the normal balance side is where the account will decrease in value. We have to take note here that the normal side is dependent on the nature of the account as illustrated below:

Account

Dr	Cr
Assets	Liabilities
	Capital

The illustration above is very much similar to the accounting equation, where Assets is equal to Liabilities and Capital. In which case, the assets' normal side is the debit side, and if there is an increase in asset, the asset account has to be debited. Correspondingly, if there is a decrease in asset, the asset account has to be credited. Thus, if there is an increase in liability or capital, the liability or capital account has to be credited. If the liability or capital account decreases, then it has to be debited.

Example 1: Increase in Asset, Increase in Liability

January 2 – The business received P20,000.25 as proceeds from bank loan.

Analysis:

The two accounts affected are:
  Cash and Loans Payable

Cash is an asset, and it increased, therefore, it is to be debited.
Loans Payable is a liability and it increased, therefore it is to be credited.

Let us discuss this with the same illustrative example we use above. First, we need to identify the accounts affected, then determine what happened to these accounts before finally arriving at a decision whether the account will be debited or credited.

As can be noted in the Example 1 above, one possible transaction can be an increase in asset which is brought about by a corresponding increase in liability. There are similar examples of this which are indicated below:

a. The business purchased office supplies on account
b. The business purchased equipment and issued a promissory note.
c. The business acquired mortgage funds on its land and building.

The analysis is difficult at first but will be later on easier with constant practice. We will have another example below:

In example, 2, another possible transaction is when an asset will increase because of a corresponding increase in capital. Similar examples are the following:

a. The owner invested cash in the business.

b. The owner used his own building as office space of the business. This becomes part of his investment.

As indicated in example 3 above, a transaction may cause one asset to increase while it decreases another asset. Similar transactions are as follows:

a. The business sold its equipment for cash.
b. The customer issued a note as payment for its account.

Another example is provided below:

Example 4: Decrease in asset, decrease in liability.

January 7– The business paid its account to a supplier

Analysis:

The two accounts affected are:
    Accounts Payable and Cash

Accounts Payable is a liability and it decreased, therefore, it is to be debited.
Cash is an asset, and it decreased, therefore it is to be credited.

As indicated above, a liability decreases while an asset decreases. This is the case when a liability is paid. Similar examples will be the payment of loans payable, salaries payable, mortgage payable, and accounts payable. In these transactions, the liability account decreases because it is paid. Correspondingly, the asset account decreases because it is used to pay the liability.

Example5: Decrease in asset, decrease in capital.

January 9– The owner withdrew office supplies for personal use.

Analysis:

The two accounts affected are:
    Owner's drawing and Supplies Inventory

Owner's drawing is a capital account and it increased. But because the drawing account is a reduction against capital, therefore, it is to be debited.
Supplies inventory is an asset, and it decreased, therefore it is to be credited.

As indicated above, an asset and capital decreased at the same time. This is normally the case when the owner of the business will withdraw assets from the enterprise for personal use.

It is also possible that liability increases while another liability decreases. This is indicated in the example below:

But how about revenue and expense accounts? How are these to be analysed?

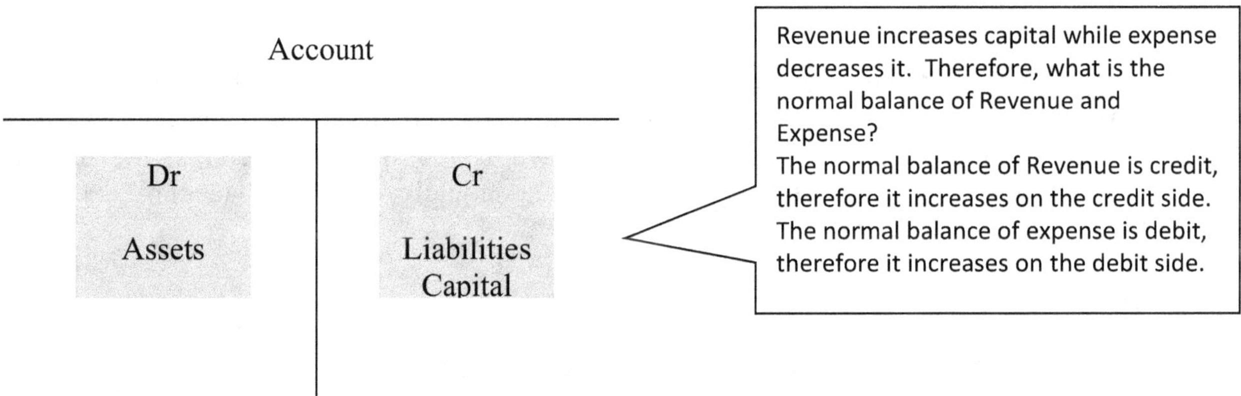

Revenue and expenses, as indicated in the Figure above, affects the T-account through its transmission channel, the capital account. As such, we can possibly analyze revenue and expense through the capital account. For example, if business rendered services, it generates revenue. Revenue increases the capital account, and the capital account increases in the credit side, therefore, revenue increases in the credit side as well. We illustrate this analysis below:

In the case of expenses, we know that expenses decrease capital, and capital decreases when it is debited. Thus, any increase in expenses will result to a decrease in capital. Therefore, an increase in expense needs to be debited. This analysis is illustrated below:

Example 8: Increase in expenses, decrease in asset.

January 15– The business paid P12,000 for workers' salaries.

Analysis:

The two accounts affected are:
    Salaries Expense and Cash

Salaries Expense increased and consequently it decreased capital. Capital decreases when debited, therefore, Salaries Expense is to be debited.
Cash decreased and it is an asset, therefore it is to be credited.

Given this, we can therefore show that the normal balance of revenue is credit, while the normal balance of expense is debit. See illustration below:

Account

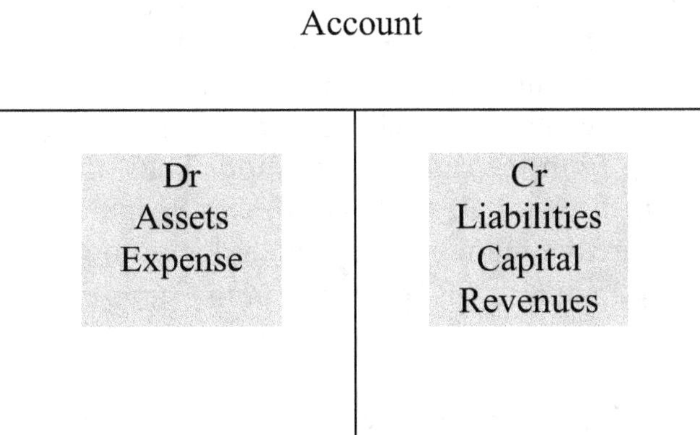

Recording transactions in the journal

The first phase of accounting, recording, involves the recording of transactions in the book of original entry referred to as the journal. The journal is an accounting devise used to record transactions chronologically, according to how it affects the accounting values – assets, liabilities, capital, revenue and expense (Cabrera et al 2010).

A journal sheet with a sample entry looks like the one presented below:

Centavos

Date		Particulars	F	Debit						Credit					
01	02	*Cash*		2	0	0	0	0	25						
		Loans Payable								2	0	0	0	0	25
		Bank loan													

The journal has at least six distinct components. These are the following:

- Date – the column where one enters the date at which the transaction occurred. This is on a month-day format. In the first column we enter the month either in number or abbreviated words (e.g. 01 or Jan). In the second column, we enter the day. In the illustration above, the date column reads as January 2.
- Particulars – this is the column where we enter the account titles affected by the transaction. In a journal entry, there is at least one debit and one credit. The debited account will be written directly after the border. The credited account is indented from the debit position. An explanation for the transaction is also presented, indented a few spaces from the credit entry. This is illustrated in the figure above.
- Folio (f) – this is a reference column, normally the page of the ledger where the entry is posted. We will get back to this in the next chapter.
- Debit – for the debit amounts. This is written starting from the rightmost part which is the place for centavos. Each column represents a place (ones, tens, hundreds, etc), starting from the rightmost portion. Thus, the debit amount above shows P20,000.25. In the journal, there is no need to put commas and decimal points as the place where the numbers are written determine its value.
- Credit – for the credit amounts, this is written in the same instruction as the debit column.

As such, journalizing involves the process of entering the transactions in the journal after we have carefully analyzed them. The analysis points discussed above will be our guide in entering the transactions into the journal. Further, to know what account titles we need to use in recording the transactions in the journal, we need to refer to an organization's chart of accounts.

An organization's chart of accounts is a listing of all account titles that the business will use in its accounting operations and in financial statement preparation. An example of a Chart of Accounts is shown below.

Code	Account Title
101	Cash
102	Accounts Receivable
103	Supplies
104	Equipment
105	Office Furniture
201	Accounts Payable
301	E. Pol, Capital
302	E. Pol, Withdrawal
401	Service Income
501	Salaries Expense
502	Taxes and Licenses
503	Rent Expense
504	Advertising Expense
505	Light and Water

Thus, when one records a transaction, he makes use of the account titles that are indicated in the Chart of Accounts. Thus, Taxes and Licenses is to be used instead of Permits and Taxes. Office Furniture is the account to be used instead of Furniture and Fixtures, if this is what is used by the business as indicated by its chart of accounts.

A Sample Problem

Below we present a list of transactions and an answer key as to how the transactions are recorded in the journal:

Transactions:

October	1	Enrico invested the following:
		Cash P20,000.00
		Equipment 5,000.00
	5	Purchased supplies P500.00 and paid cash
	7	Rendered plumbing services to customers on account, P750.00
	10	Bought additional equipment on account, P3, 000.00
	15	Paid P9,000.00 for office furniture
	16	Collected P400.00 from customers on account
	18	Received cash of P1,000.00 from various customers
	25	Made a cash withdrawal of P400.00
	30	Additional investment, P1,000.00

The following chart of account is presented.

Cash	101	Accounts Receivable	102
Supplies	103	Equipment	104
Office Furniture	105	Accounts Payable	201
E. Pol, Capital	301	E. Pol, Withdrawal	302
Service Income	401		

Answers:

Date		Particulars	Debit						Credit					
10	1	Cash	2	0	0	0	0	00						
		Equipment		5	0	0	0	00						
		E, Pol, Capital							2	5	0	0	0	00
		Initial investment												
		#												
	5	Supplies			5	0	0	00						
		Cash									5	0	0	00
		Supplies on account												
		#												
	7	Accounts Receivable			7	5	0	00						
		Service Income									7	5	0	00
		Service on account												
		#												
	10	Equipment		3	0	0	0	00						
		Accounts Payable								3	0	0	0	00
		Equipment on account												
		#												
	15	Office Furniture		9	0	0	0	00						
		Cash								9	0	0	0	00
		Furniture for cash												
		#												
	16	Cash			4	0	0	00						
		Accounts Receivable									4	0	0	00
		Collection of account												
		#												
	18	Cash		1	0	0	0	00						
		Service Income								1	0	0	0	00
		Received cash for services												
		#												
	25	E. Pol, Withdrawal			4	0	0	00						
		Cash									4	0	0	00
		Owner's Drawing												
		#												

Date		Particulars	Debit							Credit					
	30	Cash			1	0	0	0	00						
		E. Pol, Capital									1	0	0	0	00
		Additional investment													

Simple Versus Compound Journal Entries

A simple entry affects only at least two accounts or is composed of one debit and one credit. A compound entry, on the other hand affects more than two accounts, or is composed of one debit and two or more credits, two or more debits and one credit, or two or more debits and two or more credits. As such, if a transaction will result to two entries or more, we can express it in only a single entry, making it a single compound journal entry, than two simple journal entries. We illustrate this in the example below:

Transaction: Rendered services for P20,000 on January 5, 2011. A downpayment of P5,000 was paid by the customer and the remaining was on account.

In this case, we can present the journal entry as two separate simple entries as follows:

```
Jan 5 2011      Cash                    5,000
                    Service Income          5,000
                        Downpayment  for services rendered
                            #


                Accounts Receivable    15,000
                    Service Income          15,000
                        Rendered services on account
```

Instead of the above entry, we can have a single compound entry as follows:

```
Jan 5 2011      Cash                    5,000
                Accounts Receivable    15,000
                    Service Income          20,000
                        Rendered services on account with down payment
                            #
```

Given above, we have to note that the effect on the assets (cash and accounts receivable) and revenues (service income) is the same for both simple and compound entries.

We must note, however, that a compound entry can only be used for a transaction that affects several accounts, as the one indicated above. We cannot use a compound entry to summarize two or more transactions into one entry because this will make the journal entry meaningless. For example, below:

Transaction: Paid light and water bills on Jan 6 2011, P750. Rendered services for cash P1000 on the same day. The correct entry is

Jan 6 2011	*Light and Water*	*750*	
	Cash		*750*
	Paid light and water bill		
	#		
	Accounts Receivable	*1000*	
	Service Income		*1000*
	Rendered services on account		

We cannot make a compound entry for this like below:

Jan 6 2011	*Light and Water*	*750*	
	Accounts Receivable	*1000*	
	Cash		*750*
	Service Income		*1000*

The above entry is meaningless and thus cannot be validly made.

End of Chapter Activities

Exercise 4.1

Name:	Course &year:	Date:
Subject:	Time:	Score:

Discussion Questions. Individually or in groups, respond to the following requirements

1. Transaction Identification.
    a. List down transactions that would affect assets only and not any other accounting values.

    b. List down transactions that would affect liabilities only and not any other accounting values.

    c. List down transactions that would cause an increase in revenue.

    d. List down transactions that would cause an increase in expenses.

    e. List down transactions that would cause decreases in the asset accounts.

f.   List down transactions that would cause increases in the liability accounts.

g.   List down transactions that would cause increases in the capital account?

2. Value of the Journal
    a.   What do you think is the importance of using the journal?

    b.   How does the journal allow the systematic organization of financial information?

Exercise 4.2

Name:	Course &year:	Date:
Subject:	Time:	Score:

True or False. Write true if statement is true and false if otherwise. Place your answer on the blanks provided after each statement.

1. A change in asset is always accompanied by a change in liabilities and/or capital

   ____

2. Every business transaction affects no less than two accounts in the accounting equation

   ____

3. Capital increases with revenues and decreases with expenses

   ____

4. Acquisition of supplies for cash does not affect total assets

   ____

5. Purchase of supplies on account decreases assets

   ____

6. Equity refers to either creditor's or owner's equity

   ____

7. All business transaction should be entered or recorded in the journal

   ____

8. Business transactions affect the accounting equation

   ____

9. Assets are always equal to liabilities and capital

   ____

10. Notes payable differ from account payable in that the former is supported with a promissory note, while the latter is not.

    ____

11. Capital is synonymous to net worth

    ____

12. The accounting equation is the same to all forms and types of business organizations

    ____

13. Zero liabilities and P50, 000.00 capital means that all assets were provided by the creditors.

    ____

14. Withdrawal means additional investment

    ____

15. When business gets a loan from the bank, liabilities will decrease.

    ____

Exercise 4.3

Name:	Course &year:	Date:
Subject:	Time:	Score:

Identification. Indicate the normal balance of the following accounts. Write your answer on the blanks provided

1. Paig, Drawing ______	16. Furniture and Fixtures ______
2. Bonds payable ______	17. Taxes Payable ______
3. Notes Receivable ______	18. Professional Fees ______
4. Unused Supplies ______	19. Commission Income ______
5. Insurance Expense ______	20. Postage Expense ______
6. Service Income ______	21. Delivery Truck ______
7. Subscription Income ______	22. Miscellaneous Expense ______
8. Utilities Expense ______	23. Bad Debts Expense ______
9. Rent Income ______	24. Service Income ______
10. Subscription Income ______	25. SSS Contribution ______
11. Accounts Payable ______	26. Loan payable ______
12. Insurance Expense ______	27. Mortgage Payable ______
13. Cash on hand and in Bank ______	28. Utilities Payable ______
14. Interest Income ______	29. Interest Receivable ______
15. Notes payable ______	30. Mende, Capital ______

Exercise 4.4

Name:	Course &year:	Date:
Subject:	Time:	Score:

Identifying Debit and Credit. Indicate the Debit and the Credit using the following transactions. A sample is provided at the beginning.

	Debit	Credit
Example: The owner made an initial cash investment in the business.	*Cash*	*Owner's Capital*
1. Received amount borrowed from bank		
2. Additional investment in the business		
3. Cash withdrawal for personal use		
4. Bought delivery truck on account and issued a promissory note		
5. Bought machinery for cash		
6. Received cash from customers		
7. Rendered services on account		
8. Paid amount due to the bank		
9. Acquired delivery truck for cash		
10. Paid taxes and licenses		

Exercise 4.5

Name:	Course &year:	Date:
Subject:	Time:	Score:

Identifying Debit and Credit. Indicate the Debit and the Credit using the following transactions. A sample is provided at the beginning.

	Debit	Credit
Example: The owner made an initial cash investment in the business.	*Cash*	*Owner's Capital*
1. Invested equipment in the business		
2. Bough office supplies on account		
3. Rendered services to a customer and received a promissory note		
4. Borrowed money from a friend for business use		
5. Paid rent of office space		
6. Collected customer's account		
7. Rendered services for cash		
8. Paid salaries of workers		
9. Withdrew office supplies for personal use		
10. Rendered services on account		

Exercise 4.6

Name:	Course &year:	Date:
Subject:	Time:	Score:

Journalizing. Journalize the following transactions. Please use journal sheets.

Problem 1: Balik Works

Mr. Balikbayan opened a plumbing service called Balik Works. The following business transactions were completed for the month of October.

Oct	1	Balikbayan invested cash of P20,000 in the business
	5	Purchased supplies P500.00 and paid cash
	7	Rendered plumbing services to customers on account, P750.00
	10	Bought additional equipment on account, P3,000.00
	15	Paid P9,000.00 for office furniture
	16	Collected P400.00 from customers on account
	18	Received cash of P1,000.00 from various customers
	20	Paid 50% of account on October 10
	25	Made a cash withdrawal of P400.00
	30	Additional investment, P1,000.00

The following account titles should be used.

Cash	101	Accounts Payable	201
Accounts Receivable	102	Balikbayan, Capital	301
Supplies	103	Balikbayan, Withdrawal	302
Equipment	104	service Income	401
Office Furniture	105		

Use a journal sheet to answer this exercise.

Exercise 4.7

Name:	Course &year:	Date:
Subject:	Time:	Score:

Journalizing. Journalize the following transactions. Please use journal sheets.

Problem 2: Beauty Shop ni Gloria

Beauty Shop ni Gloria has the following transactions in January 2010

1	Owner invested cash in the business, P100,000
2	Purchased shop supplies on account from Drilon Co P20,000
3	Paid rent of shop space, P1750
5	Paid the amount due to Drilon
6	Paid business permits, P2,500
8	Rendered services for cash, P5,000
11	Rendered services of P2,000 on account
15	Paid salaries to workers, P4,000
19	Rendered services to various customers for cash P5,600
22	Paid light and water bills, P450
23	Owner withdrew cash from the business – P500
29	Collected in full the account of customers on January 11
30	Paid salaries of workers, P3,800

The following account titles should be used.

Cash	101	Accounts Payable	201
Accounts Receivable	102	Gloria, Capital	301
Shop Supplies	103	Gloria, Drawing	302
Equipment	104	Service Income	401
		Light and Water	501
		Rent Expense	502
		Salaries Expense	503
		Taxes and Licenses	504

Use a journal sheet to answer this exercise.

Exercise 4.8

Name:	Course &year:	Date:
Subject:	Time:	Score:

Journalizing. Journalize the following transactions. Please use journal sheets.

Problem 3: CJ Laundry

Ms. ChrisJul owns a self-service laundry shop. She started the business in January and the following business transactions occurred during the month. The laundry shop operates on a cash basis.

Jan   1   ChrisJul invested the following:

Washing Machine + Dryer	P450,000
Detergent and Fabric Softener	20,000
Tables and Chairs	80,000
Money	50,000

    2   Received P3,200 from various customers for laundry services
    3   Received P2,900 from various customers for laundry services
    5   Received P1,800 from various customers for laundry services
    7   Paid 2,400 salaries of workers for the week
    8   Bought additional dryer on account for P40,000
  12   Received cash of P3,200.00 from various customers
  14   Paid 60% of account on January 8
  18   Received cash from various customers for services
  22   ChrisJul withdrew P5,000 cash from the business
  24   Paid light and water bill, P4,600
  30   Paid salaries of workers for 3 weeks P8,600

The following account titles should be used.

Cash	Accounts Payable
Laundry Supplies	ChrisJul, Capital
Laundry Equipment	ChrisJul, Withdrawal
Shop Furniture	Service Income
Office Furniture	Light and Water
	Salaries Expense

GROUP WORK

Go back to the results of the exercise that you did in the last chapter. Record the transactions that you have identified in the journal. Transfer your answers in manila paper and present in the class.

Annex to Chapter 4: Business Forms and Journal Entries

In this attachment to the chapter, business forms and how these business forms become journal entries in the books of accounts are presented. The reason why these are presented is to give students a view of how transactions are captured by source documents and how these are translated into actual journal entries in the books of accounts.

Source documents are business forms that capture the essence of a business transaction. Source documents are normally business forms designed by its primary user. For example, an official receipt, a source document which is a proof that cash is received by the business, is designed by the business who receives the cash. In this case, there can be two types of source documents. The first one is internal, which refers to those documents developed by the business and for use within the business itself. An example of this is a liquidation report, which shows the money received by an employee of a business and a report as to how this was used.

In most cases, we record transactions in the journal by referring to a source document that captures the essence of the transaction. In this case, we present the samples below:

Official Receipt (revenue)

STEP UP CONSULTING SERVICES
3 Genaro Visarra St., Tagbilaran City, 6300 Bohol Philippines
Proprietor: Michael P. Cañares
TIN # 179-933-138-000 NON-VAT
(038)5019210/ 09209107972

OR Number 0103
Date Sept. 17, 2010
(*This serves as your official receipt.*)

Name of Client : DTI - Bohol
Address : Tagb. City

Received from the above named person the amount of Eight thousand seven hundred pesos
(P 8,700.00) as payment of the following services rendered to the latter, the details of which are as follows:

Service Description	Duration	Amount
PF during the FGD on Value Chain for Coffee Industry	July 7-8, 2010	P 8,700.00
	TOTAL	P 8,700.00

Printed by: LOU-BETH Printing Press - 47 Burjos St., Tagbilaran City, Bohol   RD 084-1000-04   50 bklts.   0001-2500   07-27-2004
TIN # 129-159-434-000

Received by: _______________

An official receipt is a form which documents cash received by the business from a customer. In the above example, we can see that Step Up Consulting Services received money in the total amount of P8,700 as professional fees for the conduct a of training. The amount is received on 17 September 2010 from customer DTI. Note that the official receipt is prenumbered and is used in a sequence. To enhance integrity, these receipts need to be regularly audited so as to ensure that all cash received by the business is actually recorded in the books of accounts.

How is the above transaction recorded in the books of accounts?

We present below the suggested journal entry to record this transaction:

<u>Nature of transaction: Received cash for services rendered:</u>

Sept 17, 2010   Cash   8,700
                              Service Income   8,700
                                    To record income from services rendered.

In the above, it is assumed that Step Up Consulting Services is the business, thus its official receipt is a proof of income or revenue.

However, if an official receipt is received by the business as payment for availed goods or services, it is not a revenue receipt, but an expense receipt. This is indicated in the discussion below.

Official Receipt (expense)

When a business pays an expense, the business also receives an official receipt. In this case, it is not a revenue receipt but rather an expense receipt. This is illustrated below:

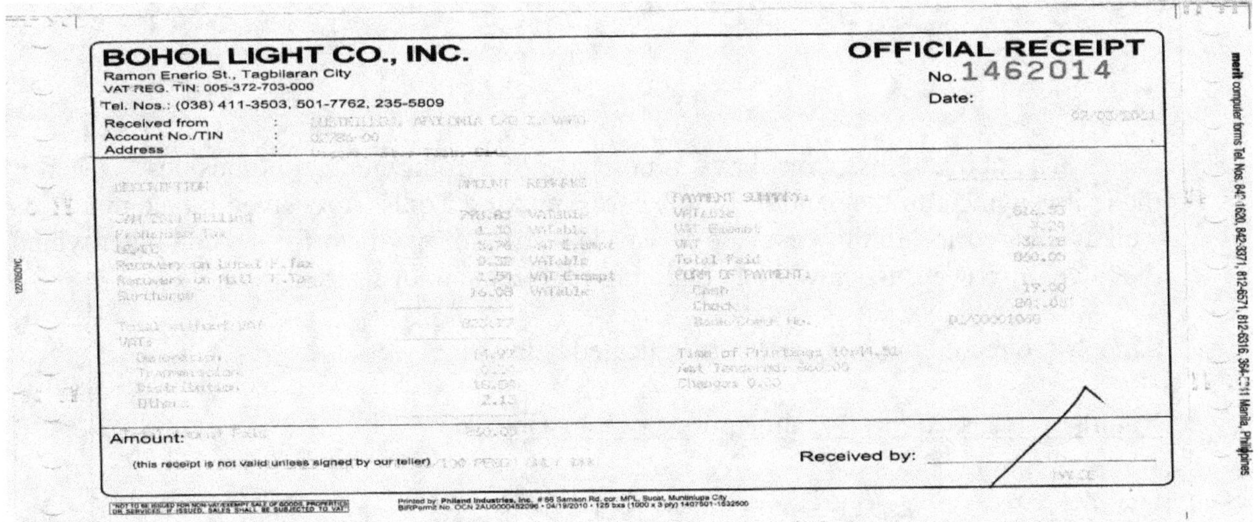

The receipt above is not a proof of revenue on the part of Step Up but a proof of paid expense. In this case, Step Up paid light and water to Bohol Light Company, Inc for the month of January 2011. When Step Up paid, it received a receipt as a proof of payment. The above transaction is recorded in the books of accounts using the following entry:

Nature of Transaction: Payment for electric bill

Feb 3, 2011   Light and Water   841.05
                    Cash   841.05
                        To record payment of electric bill.

Official Receipt (purchase of an asset)

If a business also purchases asset, it also receives an official receipt. An example of this type is given below:

OFFICIAL RECEIPT

THINKING-TOOLS
Island City Mall, Dampas District
Tagbilaran City, Bohol 6300
Tel. Nos. 501-7808 to 10
Fax No. 501-7807
TIN-000-312-081-006-VAT

No. 17261

Date 11 / 15 20 10

Received from MICHAEL CANARES
with Address at ___________ TIN ___________
the sum of ___________ (P 26,999.20)

APPLICATION OF PAYMENT		FORM OF PAYMENT	
INVOICE NOS.	AMOUNT	CHECKS	AMOUNT
Full payment for 1 unit Desktop Pc	26,999.20	ALLIED BANK / MC 5757 4215 0007 5676	
Valable Sale			
VAT		CASH ☐	
TOTAL ₱	26,999.20	TOTAL ₱	

Payment received by:

The above transaction shows a purchase of a computer by the business. When it made its payment to the vendor, in this case Thinking Tools, it received the computer as well as this receipt. In this case, the receipt is a proof of payment for the computer which the buyer also needs to show when claiming replacement, or warranty.

An entry to record this transaction is indicated below:

Nature of Transaction: Bought equipment for cash:

Nov 15, 2010   Equipment   26,999.20
                    Cash   26,999.20
                        To record purchase of equipment.

Payroll Sheet

A payroll sheet is a summary of hours worked by and equivalent payment to each employee for a pay period. The payroll sheet is a form, when approved by appropriate authority, will become the basis for the payment of salaries. A sample of a payroll sheet is shown below:

Step Up Consulting Services
3 G. Visarra Street, Tagbilaran City

PAYROLL SHEET
March 16-31, 2011

Employee		Basic Rate				NET
		days work	rate per day			PAY
Hedz Paredes		7	500.00	regular	3,500.00	
		6	1,000.00	fieldwork	6,000.00	**9,500.00**
Lotty Sale		8.5	255.00	regular	2,167.50	
		3	300.00	fieldwork	900.00	**3,067.50**
		SSS	183.30			
		Philhealth	62.50			
		Pag-ibig	100.00		345.80	**2,721.70**
				Total		**12,567.50**

The above form tells us of the number of days worked by the employees, the amount of payment per employee on a particular pay period and deductions for mandated obligations. Needless to say, a payroll sheet is a confidential document.

This sheet, however, does not give authority to pay the salary. Only when this is approved that salary will be paid. As such, at this point, there is no journal entry yet. It is only when disbursement authorization is done through another document that a journal entry can be done. This is discussed below.

Cash Disbursement Voucher/Check Disbursement Voucher

A cash/check disbursement voucher is a form that authorizes a payment of a particular expense item like salaries, utilities, or even the purchase of supplies and equipment. As such, before we can actually pay a supplier of goods or service, we first get an authorization for it. The authorization is in the form of this voucher.

In most vouchers, a journal entry is already indicated, however, the amount of cash is only equal to the amount that will actually be disbursed by the business. A sample is presented below:

<table>
<tr><td colspan="2">STEP UP CONSULTING SERVICES
3 Genaro Visarra St., Tagbilaran</td><td colspan="2">Cash Disbursement Voucher
No. <u>00888</u>
Date <u>03/31/2011</u></td></tr>
<tr><td colspan="4">Pay to: Lotty Sale</td></tr>
</table>

Particulars	Amount
Salaries for the period (March 16-31, 2011)	Php12,221.70

Approved for payment:

____

Received payment :

____

Journal Entry

Date	Particulars	Debit	Credit
3/31/2011	Salaries and Wages	12,567.50	
	SSS Payable		183.30
	PHIC Payable		62.50
	HDMF Payable		100.00
	Cash in bank		12,221.70

The journal entry is already indicated above. Note that the payee for the salaries in this case is one of those to whom salary is paid because she is the administrative and disbursing officer of the organization.

In this case also, the journal entry is composed of one debit and four credits. This is what we refer to as a compound entry indicated also somewhere else in this chapter.

The above are just examples of business forms and how these captures the essence of business transactions. The above examples also illustrate to us how business forms facilitate the preparation of journal entries.

Chapter 5. Classifying Transactions Through the Ledger

At the end of the chapter the student is expected to:

a. Know the procedures in posting transactions to the ledger.
b. Know and understand the proper use of ledger.
c. Appreciate the process of posting transactions to the ledger.
d. Know the mechanics of footing the ledger.
e. Actualize skills on footing and trial balance preparation.

The diagram below, which appears in the previous chapter, shows the four phases of accounting. In Chapter 4, we learned about how to record transactions in the journal, which is essentially the first phase in accounting. In this chapter, we shall move on to the second phase which is about classification of transactions.

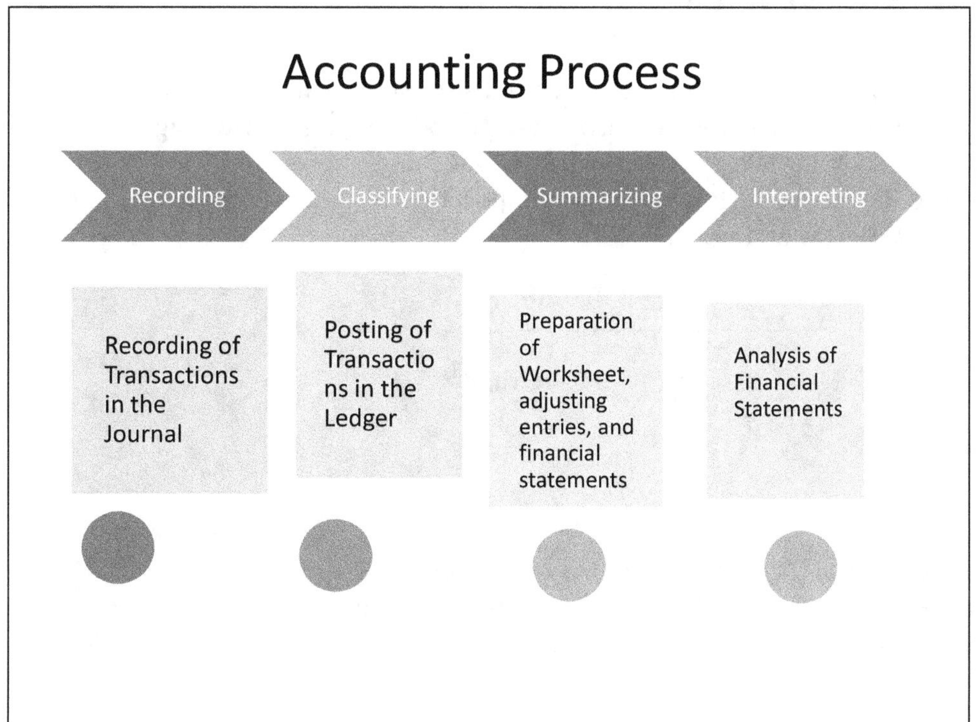

Classifying is an accounting process of grouping together transaction effects to the same types of financial statement accounts. In this case, the bases of the classifying phase are the journal entries that were recorded. Needless to say, when the journal entries are wrong, it follows that the classification will also be wrong and therefore meaningless, as it would not render an accurate presentation of the business' financial position or results of operations. Essentially, classifying involves the posting of the recorded transactions in the ledger, considered the book of final entry.

Each transaction affects at least two accounts, as what we have learned in the previous chapter. Businesses, however, do not only have a single transaction in a day. Transactions can be as many depending on the size of the company, the nature of its products, and the volume of its customers. Also, an account can be positively (meaning, the account will increase) or negatively (the account will decrease) affected by a transaction. In this case, there is a need to know all the effects of the business transactions to particular accounts in a certain period.

For example, we purchased office supplies at least 20 times in a given month, how do we know the total of all office supplies purchased for the month?

The only way to know this is to classify the effects of transactions on a per account basis. Thus, we need to have transaction effects posted to each account. This is the process of posting.

How do we post transactions?

As what we have learned in the previous chapter, a T-Account is an accounting tool used to summarize the transactions for a particular period of time affecting a certain accounting value or account. We also knew that a T-account is prepared for all accounts of a business. The T- Account, however, is composed of 2 sides – the debit, and the credit side and this is illustrated below:

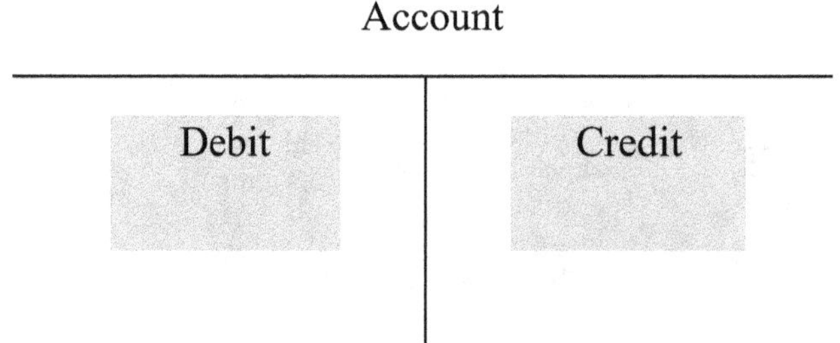

In this case, we need to prepare one T-account for each of the accounts contained in a business's chart of accounts so that we will be able to summarize all transactions that affect each of the accounts in a particular period. As an example, we use the following list of transactions, abstracted from the previous chapter's problems that affect the cash accounts.

> October   1 Enrico invested the following:
>   Cash   P20, 000.00
>   5 Purchased supplies P500.00 and paid cash
>   17 Collected P400.00 from customers on account
>   18 Received cash of P1, 000.00 from various customers
>   26 Made a cash withdrawal of P400.00
>   31 Additional investment, P1, 000.00

If we want to summarize the effect of the above transactions to the cash account, one option is to do a simple mathematical computation as indicated below:

Cash received:	
Oct 1 – investment	P20,000.00
Oct 15 – collections	400.00
Oct 18 – sales from various customers	1,000.00
Oct 30 – additional investment	1,000.00
Total Cash Received	P22,400.00
Less: Cash paid	
Oct 5 – purchase of supplies P 500.00	
Oct 25 – cash withdrawal 400.00	900.00
Cash balance for October	P21,500.00

However, the T account is a more convenient device in doing this summary. As such, if this accounting tool is used, it will look like this:

Cash

10/1 investment	20,000	10/5 office supplies	500
10/15 collections	400	10/25 owner's drawing	400
10/18 sales	1,000		
10/30 investment	1,000		
Total debits	22,400	Total Credits	900
Balance	**21,500**		

The Ledger

To facilitate the preparation of the summary of each account through the use of the T account as indicated in the example above, we introduce in this chapter the ledger which is considered the book of final entry (Weygandt et al 2015). The ledger summarizes the journal entries affecting each account in a given accounting period and resembles exactly a T- account. There are two sides of a ledger, the debit and the credit side. Each side has a date, particulars, folio and amount columns where journal entries will be transferred for purposes of classification. The ledger looks like the form presented below:

Account							
Date	Particulars	F	Amount	Date	Particulars	F	Amount

As earlier mentioned, the ledger has two sides, the debit side and the credit side. Each side has the following components:

a. Date – the date at which the transaction occurred. On the first column, we write here the number equivalent of the month (e.g. 10 for October). On the second column, we write here the date when the transaction happened.
b. Particulars – this is the space where we shall write the nature of the transaction that happened on this date. In other accounting practice, this is where the corresponding credit (if the account is debited) or debit (if the account is credited) is written. For example, if cash is received by crediting sales, sales is written on the particulars section of the cash account
c. Folio – the corresponding journal page where the account posted come from as handy reference. For example, if the entry comes from the 2nd page of the journal, one may write J-002. Also, in the journal, the folio indicates also the page where the transaction is posted in the ledger. We will illustrate this in an example below.
d. Amount – the peso amount of the transaction posted. The same rule applies regarding where the figures will be positioned in the columns like that indicated in the previous chapter.

Example

As an example, we shall use the transactions journalized in the previous chapter. The journal is illustrated again below for handy reference. Please take note that this time around, we already indicated the folio entries in the journal.

Date		Particulars		Debit							Credit					
10	1	Cash	L-1	2	0	0	0	0	00							
		Equipment	l-4		5	0	0	0	00							
		E. Pol. Capital	l-7								2	5	0	0	0	00
		Initial investment														
		#														
	5	Supplies	l-3			5	0	0	00							
		Cash	L-1										5	0	0	00
		Supplies for cash														
		#														
	7	Accounts Receivable	l-2			7	5	0	00							
		Service Income	l-9										7	5	0	00
		Service on account														
		#														
	10	Equipment	L-4		3	0	0	0	00							
		Accounts Payable	L-6									3	0	0	0	00
		Equipment on account														
		#														
	15	Office Furniture	L-5		9	0	0	0	00							
		Cash	l-1									9	0	0	0	00
		Furniture for cash														
		#														
	16	Cash	l-1			4	0	0	00							
		Accounts Receivable	l-2										4	0	0	00
		Collection of account														
		#														
	18	Cash	l-1		1	0	0	0	00							
		Service Income	l-9									1	0	0	0	00
		Received cash for services														
		#														
	25	E. Pol. Withdrawal	l-8			4	0	0	00							
		Cash	l-1										4	0	0	00
		Owner's Drawing														
		#														
	30	Cash	l-1		1	0	0	0	00							
		E. Pol. Capital										1	0	0	0	00
		Additional investment														

The transactions are posted below:

CASH — 001

Date		Particulars	F	Amount						Date		Particulars	F	Amount					
10	1	Investment	j-1	2	0	0	0	0	00	10	5	Supplies	j-1				5	0	0	00
	16	Collection	j-1			4	0	0	00		15	Furniture	j-1		9	0	0	0	00
	18	Service income	j-1		1	0	0	0	00		25	Drawing	j-1			4	0	0	00
	30	Investment	j-1		1	0	0	0	00						9	9	0	0	00
				2	2	4	0	0	00										
		12,500 bal																	

ACCOUNTS RECEIVABLE — 002

Date		Particulars	F	Amount					Date		Particulars	F	Amount			
10	7	Income	j-1		7	5	0	00	10	16	Collection	j-1		4	0	0	00
		350 bal															

SUPPLIES — 003

Date		Particulars	F	Amount					Date		Particulars	F	Amount
10	5	Purchase	j-1		5	0	0	00					
		500 bal											

EQUIPMENT — 004

Date		Particulars	F	Amount						Date		Particulars	F	Amount
10	1	Investment	j-1		5	0	0	0	00					
	10	Purchase	j-1		3	0	0	0	00					
		8000 bal												

OFFICE FURNITURE — 005

Date		Particulars	F	Amount						Date		Particulars	F	Amount
10	15	Purchase	j-1		9	0	0	0	00					
		9000 bal												

ACCOUNTS PAYABLE — 006

Date		Particulars	F	Amount						Date		Particulars	F	Amount					
										10	10	Equipment	j-1			3	0	0	0	00

E. POL. CAPITAL — 007

Date		Particulars	F	Amount						Date		Particulars	F	Amount						
										10	1	Investment	j-1		2	5	0	0	0	00
											30	Investment	j-1		1	0	0	0	0	00
												26000 bal								

E. POL, WITHDRAWAL   008

Date		Particulars	F	Amount							Date		Particulars	F	Amount						
10	25	Cash drawing	J-1				4	0	0	00											

SERVICE INCOME   009

Date		Particulars	F	Amount							Date		Particulars	F	Amount						
											10	7	Cash income	j-1				7	5	0	00
												18	Cash income	j-1			1	0	0	0	00
													1750 bal								

As can be seen above, classifying constitutes primarily the transfer of journal entries from the journal to the ledger. There is no further analysis undertaken. What is written in the journal is transferred to the ledger, summarizing the effects of each transaction to every account of the business.

Thus, we can say that when journal entries are not properly made, it will affect the integrity of the ledger. Bookkeepers, or those who record transactions need to be very precise in journalizing because the journal entries are the main basis for the posting of accounts to the ledger.

End of Chapter Exercises

Exercise 5.1

Name:	Course &year:	Date:
Subject:	Time:	Score:

Discussion Questions. Individually, or as a group, answer the following questions.

a. How does accounting classify transactions? How does this manner of classifying transactions help users of financial information?

b. Why do you think is the ledger called the book of final entry?

c. What accounts will normally increase balance when debited?

d. What accounts will increase its balance when credited?

Exercise 5.2.

Name:	Course &year:	Date:
Subject:	Time:	Score:

Multiple Choice.   Select the best answer for each of the items. Encircle the letter of the answer that corresponds to your choice.

1. Which of the following statements is correct?
   a. Liabilities is capital invested by the owner
   b. Accounts receivable and notes receivable are the same
   c. Total assets are provided by the owner, by the creditors, or by both.
   d. None of the above
2. The account that increases with investments and decreases with withdrawal is
   a. Capital   c. Cash
   b. Notes Payable   d. Accounts Receivable
3. Payment of expenses would
   a. Increase cash and decrease payables
   b. Increase expenses and decrease cash
   c. Increase payable and decreases cash
   d. Have no effect on the business account
4. The additional investment of an owner will
   a. Increase an asset and liability account
   b. Decrease an asset and a liability account
   c. Decrease one liability and increase another liability account
   d. None of the responses
5. Which of the following transactions increase capital?
   a. Bought land for cash
   b. Bought equipment on account and issued a promissory note
   c. Rendered services on account
   d. Received cash proceeds from bank for amount borrowed
6. What is the effect upon the total assets of a business when a notes payable is paid?
   a. Increases total assets   c. no change
   b. Decreased total assets   d. none of the above
7. If a transaction causes total assets to decrease but does not affect the owner's equity, what change, if any, will occur in total liabilities?
   a. Liabilities will increase   c. Liabilities will decrease
   b. No change   d. None of the above
8. Acquisition of equipment in cash would
   a. Increase one asset account and decrease another asset account
   b. Have zero effect on the total assets
   c. Have no effect on the equity side
   d. All the responses
9. Which of the following transactions decrease capital?
   a. Bought equipment on account

    b. Rendered services for cash

    c. Paid expenses

    d. Received cash proceeds of bank loan

10. Posting is the process of
    a. Transferring the entries in the journal to the ledger
    b. Using the ledger
    c. Summarizing transactions on a per account basis
    d. All of these

11. Which among the following transactions will decrease cash?
    a. Owner's drawing   c. sales on account
    b. Rendered service for cash   d. none of these

12. Which among the following transactions will increase and decrease total assets at the same time?
    a. Purchase of office supplies on account
    b. Rendering of services for cash
    c. Collection of accounts receivable
    d. None of these

13. Statement 1: Transaction dates are only used in making journal entries.
    Statement 2: The ledger can replace the journal in accounting for transactions.
    a. Both statements are true   c. Only statement 2 is true
    b. Both statements are false   d. Only statement 1 is true.

14. Statement 1: For every debit entry in the ledger, there is always a corresponding credit entry in another account.
    Statement 2: Every account has either a debit or a credit balance in the ledger.
    a. Both statements are true   c. Only statement 2 is true
    b. Both statements are false   d. Only statement 1 is true.

15. If an expense is incurred and paid by the business, what accounts will be affected in the ledger?
    a. An asset and an expense account   c. An expense and a liability account
    b. A capital and an asset account   d. None of these

Exercise 5.3

Name:		Course &year:	Date:
Subject:		Time:	Score:

Ledger reparation. Using the transactions below, prepare the ledger of Bulaklak Flower Shoppe.

Date		Particulars	Debit	Credit
2010				
12	1	CASH	80000	
		FURNITURE AND FIXTURES	10000	
		BUWAK, CAPITAL		90000
		#		
	3	TAXES AND LICENSES	1500	
		CASH		1500
		#		
	9	ACCOUNTS RECEIVABLE	20550	
		SERVICE INCOME		20550
		#		
	11	FLORAL SUPPLIES EXPENSE	4500	
		ACCOUNTS PAYABLE		4500
		#		
	16	CASH	9000	
		SERVICE INCOME		9000
		#		
	17	CASH	10400	
		ACCOUNTS RECEIVABLE		10400
		#		
	20	ACCOUNTS PAYABLE	1000	
		CASH		1000
		#		
	22	CASH	50000	
		LOANS PAYABLE		50000
		PAYMENT OF ACCOUNTS		
		#		
	24	BUWAK, WITHDRAWAL	7500	
		CASH		7500
		#		
	30	CASH	10000	
		BUWAK, CAPITAL		10000
		#		
	31	SALARIES EXPENSE	5500	
		CASH		5500

Exercise 5.4

Name:	Course &year:	Date:
Subject:	Time:	Score:

Fill in the blanks. Fill in the blanks with the correct answer.

Sample:

Transaction	Ledger accounts affected	Which side?
Owner invested cash in the business	Cash	Debit
	Capital	Credit

	Transaction	**Ledger accounts affected**	**Which side?**
1	Paid rent expense	_______________	_______________
		_______________	_______________
2	Collected customer's account	_______________	_______________
		_______________	_______________
3	Owner withdrew cash from the business	_______________	_______________
		_______________	_______________
4	Received cash for services rendered	_______________	_______________
		_______________	_______________
5	Bough equipment on account	_______________	_______________
		_______________	_______________
6	Paid salaries of workers	_______________	_______________
		_______________	_______________
7	Rendered services on account	_______________	_______________
		_______________	_______________
8	Paid its loan from the bank	_______________	_______________
		_______________	_______________

Transaction	**Ledger accounts affected**	**Which side?**
9 Owner invested cash in the business	_____________________	_____________________
	_____________________	_____________________
10 Purchased office supplies for cash	_____________________	_____________________
	_____________________	_____________________

Exercise 5.5

Name:	Course &year:	Date:
Subject:	Time:	Score:

Journal to Ledger Exercise. Using the following transactions, prepare the journal and the ledger afterwards. As these transactions have already been answered in the previous chapter, use the correct answers in the previous chapter to prepare the ledger.

Problem 1: Balik Works

Mr. Balikbayan opened a plumbing service called Balik Works. The following business transactions were completed for the month of October.

Oct	1	Balikbayan invested cash of P20,000 in the business
	5	Purchased supplies P500.00 and paid cash
	7	Rendered plumbing services to customers on account, P750.00
	10	Bought additional equipment on account, P3,000.00
	15	Paid P9,000.00 for office furniture
	16	Collected P400.00 from customers on account
	18	Received cash of P1,000.00 from various customers
	20	Paid 50% of account on October 10
	25	Made a cash withdrawal of P400.00
	30	Additional investment, P1,000.00

The following account titles should be used.

Cash	101	Accounts Payable	201
Accounts Receivable	102	Balikbayan, Capital	301
Supplies	103	Balikbayan, Withdrawal	302
Equipment	104	service Income	401
Office Furniture	105		

Journalize the above transactions and prepare the ledger.

Exercise 5.6

Name:	Course &year:	Date:
Subject:	Time:	Score:

Journal to Ledger Exercise. Using the following transactions, prepare the journal and the ledger afterwards. As these transactions have already been answered in the previous chapter, use the correct answers in the previous chapter to prepare the ledger.

Problem 2: Beauty Shop ni Gloria

Beauty Shop ni Gloria has the following transactions in January 2010
1   Owner invested cash in the business, P100,000
2   Purchased shop supplies on account from Drilon Co P20,000
3   Paid rent of shop space, P1750
5   Paid the amount due to Drilon
6   Paid business permits, P2,500
8   Rendered services for cash, P5,000
11   Rendered services of P2,000 on account
15   Paid salaries to workers, P4,000
19   Rendered services to various customers for cash P5,600
22   Paid light and water bills, P450
23   Owner withdrew cash from the business – P500
29   Collected in full the account of customers on January 11
30   Paid salaries of workers, P3,800

The following account titles should be used:

Cash	101	Accounts Payable	201
Accounts Receivable	102	Gloria, Capital	301
Shop Supplies	103	Gloria, Drawing	302
Equipment	104	Service Income	401
		Light and Water	501
		Rent Expense	502
		Salaries Expense	503
		Taxes and Licenses	504

Journalize the above transactions and prepare the ledger.

Exercise 5.7

Name:	Course &year:	Date:
Subject:	Time:	Score:

Journal to Ledger Exercise. Using the following transactions, prepare the journal and the ledger afterwards. As these transactions have already been answered in the previous chapter, use the correct answers in the previous chapter to prepare the ledger.

Problem 3: CJ Laundry

Ms. ChrisJul owns a self-service laundry shop. She started the business in January and the following business transactions occurred during the month. The laundry shop operates on a cash basis.

Jan	1	ChrisJul invested the following:

        Washing Machine + Dryer   P450,000
        Detergent and Fabric Softener   20,000
        Tables and Chairs   80,000
        Money   50,000

- 2   Received P3,200 from various customers for laundry services
- 3   Received P2,900 from various customers for laundry services
- 5   Received P1,800 from various customers for laundry services
- 7   Paid 2,400 salaries of workers for the week
- 8   Bought additional dryer on account for P40,000
- 12   Received cash of P3,200.00 from various customers
- 14   Paid 60% of account on January 8
- 18   Received cash from various customers for services
- 22   ChrisJul withdrew P5,000 cash from the business
- 24   Paid light and water bill, P4,600
- 30   Paid salaries of workers for 3 weeks P8,600

The following account titles should be used.

Cash	Accounts Payable
Laundry Supplies	ChrisJul, Capital
Laundry Equipment	ChrisJul, Withdrawal
Shop Furniture	Service Income
Office Furniture	Light and Water
	Salaries Expense

GROUP WORK

Go back to the journal entries of your chosen business that you did in the last chapter. Post the journal entries you have made in the ledger. Compute the balance of each of the accounts posted. Show your work to the class.

Chapter 6. Preparing Financial Statements

At the end of the chapter the student is expected to:
a. Know and understand the trial balance and its use.
b. Know the mechanics of preparing the trial balance to summarize effects of transactions to account titles or values
c. Know and understand the mechanics of financial statement preparation.
d. Appreciate the importance of preparing financial statements.
e. Actualize skills in preparing financial statements.

We go back to the diagram below, presented in every beginning of the last two chapters. In Chapter 5, we discussed the importance and mechanics of classifying financial statements. In this chapter, we discuss how we prepare financial statements based on the results of the ledger.

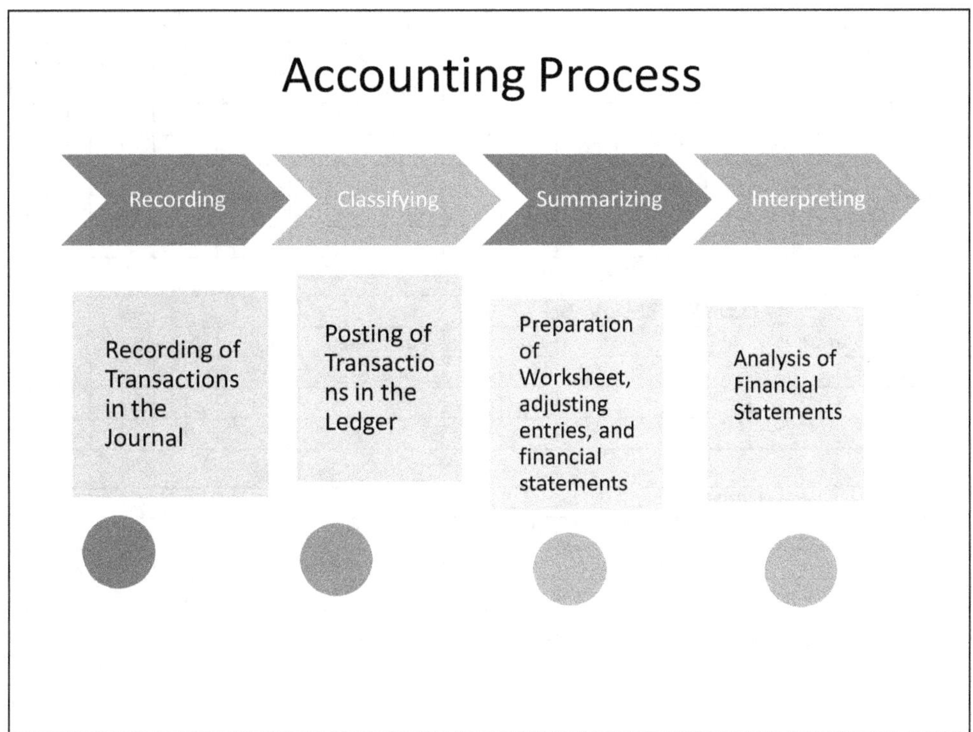

The Trial Balance

The trial balance is a summary report that shows the balances of open ledger accounts (Kimwell 2007). By open accounts, we mean, those accounts in the general ledger which balances are not yet reduced to zero. The trial balance, therefore, gives us a snap view of the different accounts and amounts of the business as of a given period of time.

The trial balance can be prepared using two approaches – the trial balance of totals, and the trial balance of balances. The trial balance of totals is a trial balance that shows the total of the debit and the credit columns of each of the accounts in the ledger (Edmonds et al 2014). The trial balance of balances, on the other hand, only shows the balance of the figures shown in the ledger, meaning, the difference between the debit and credit amounts (Ballada 2008). In this chapter, we use the trial balance of balances instead of the trial balance of totals.

We go back to the ledger prepared in Chapter 5. This will become the basis in the preparation of the trial balance. The ledger, with the corresponding details are reproduced below:

The above transactions are posted below:

CASH   001

Date		Particulars	F	Amount						Date		Particulars	F	Amount					
10	1	Investment	j-1	2	0	0	0	0	00	10	5	Supplies	j-1			5	0	0	00
	16	Collection	j-2			4	0	0	00		15	Furniture	j-1		9	0	0	0	00
	18	Service income	j-2		1	0	0	0	00		25	Drawing	j-2			4	0	0	00
	30	Investment	j-2		1	0	0	0	00						9	9	0	0	00
				2	2	4	0	0	00										
		12,500 bal																	

ACCOUNTS RECEIVABLE   002

Date		Particulars	F	Amount						Date		Particulars	F	Amount					
10	7	Income	j-1			7	5	0	00	10	16	Collection	j-2			4	0	0	00
		350 bal																	

SUPPLIES   003

Date		Particulars	F	Amount						Date		Particulars	F	Amount					
10	5	Purchase	j-1			5	0	0	00										
		500 bal																	

		EQUIPMENT								004									
Date		Particulars	F	Amount						Date		Particulars	F	Amount					
10	1	Investment	j-1			5	0	0	0	00									
	10	Purchase	j-1			3	0	0	0	00									
		8000 bal																	

		OFFICE FURNITURE								005									
Date		Particulars	F	Amount						Date		Particulars	F	Amount					
10	15	Purchase	j-1			9	0	0	0	00									
		9000 bal																	

		ACCOUNTS PAYABLE								006									
Date		Particulars	F	Amount						Date		Particulars	F	Amount					
										10	10	Equipment	j-1			3	0	0	0	00

		E. POL. CAPITAL								007									
Date		Particulars	F	Amount						Date		Particulars	F	Amount					
										10	1	Investment	j-1		2	5	0	0	0	00
											30	Investment	j-2		1	0	0	0	0	00
												26000 bal							

		E. POL, WITHDRAWAL								008									
Date		Particulars	F	Amount						Date		Particulars	F	Amount					
10	25	Cash drawing				4	0	0	00										

		SERVICE INCOME								009									
Date		Particulars	F	Amount						Date		Particulars	F	Amount					
										10	7	Cash income	j-1			7	5	0	00
											18	Cash income	j-2		1	0	0	0	00
												1750 bal							

Based on the above amounts, we will be able to prepare the trial balance. The prepared trial balance is shown below:

123

Enrico Pol

Trial Balance

October 30, 2017

Account Title	Debit	Credit
Cash	12,500.00	
Accounts Receivable	350.00	
Supplies	500.00	
Equipment	8,000.00	
Office Furniture	9,000.00	
Accounts Payable		3,000.00
E. Pol, Capital		26,000.00
E. Pol, Drawing	400.00	
Service Income		1,750.00
Totals	30,750.00	30,750.00

As can be noted from above, the trial balance preparation consists of several steps:

a. Supplying the header or the title of the report. In this case, the header consists of three lines. The first line is the name of the business (or the proprietor, in this case), followed by the title of the report (Trial Balance) and the date of the report which normally corresponds to the last day of the transaction for the month.

b. Arrange the account titles according to the following order – assets, liabilities, capital, revenue, and expense. Extract the balances from the ledger and write them on the appropriate column (either debit or credit).

c. Total the entries on the debit and the credit columns. A correctly prepared trial balance is initially indicated by the same debit and credit totals, though not necessarily an absolute assurance that the trial balance is correct.

The Financial Statements

The accounting standards mentions at least six components of financial statements. We will only deal with three basic financial statements in this chapter:

1. Income Statement

   The income statement is currently known as the Statement of Financial Operations, or Statement of Comprehensive Income. This practically shows the results of operations of the business for a period of time.

As earlier indicated when revenues exceed expenses, there is a net income but when expenses exceed revenues, there is a net loss.

2. Balance Sheet

    The Balance Sheet, currently known as Statement of Financial Position shows the financial condition of a business as of a given period of time. It tells us how much assets, liabilities, and capital, the business has as of a particular period.

3. Statement of Changes in Equity

    The Statement of Changes in Equity is a statement that presents the changes in the capital account. These changes can be additional investments, income or loss, and withdrawals.

    We do not present in this chapter the statement of cash flows.

Preparing the Financial Statements

We prepare the financial statements in the following order:

> a. We prepare first the trial balance. The trial balance is the basis in our preparation of financial statements.
> b. First, we prepare the income statement. The end figure of the income statement, which is net income, is needed to prepare the statement of changes in equity.
> c. Secondly, we prepare the statement of changes in equity. As earlier mentioned, we need the net income figure to be able to prepare this statement.
> d. Finally, we prepare the balance sheet. In preparing the balance sheet, we need the ending capital balance from the statement of changes in equity. This is the reason why we prepare this last.

In the succeeding pages, we prepare the financial statements from a pre-prepared trial balance of Ed Go, a consultant.

ED GO
Trial Balance
March 31, 2017

ACCOUNT TITLES	Debit	Credit
Cash	52,767.00	
Accounts Receivable	19,410.00	
Office Supplies	525.00	
Prepaid Insurance	6,600.00	
Prepaid Rent	6,000.00	
Office Equipment	8,505.00	
Accounts Payable		6,750.00
Ed, Capital		75,000.00
Ed, Withdrawal	4,248.00	
Consulting Fees		48,000.00
Commission Expense	7,500.00	
Salary Expense	18,000.00	
Travel and Entertainment	3,975.00	
Advertising	1,147.50	
Utilities	1,072.50	
	129,750.00	129,750.00

We prepare the income statement in the next page by clearly identifying the revenues and expenses. We have to note that only Consulting Fees and the different expenses can be considered in the preparation of the income statement, as the income statement will show the revenues and the expenses only. As the main logic of the income statement is to arrive at net income or loss, we deduct from consulting fees the various expenses to arrive at net income. Please see the illustration in the succeeding page:

ED GO
Income Statement
for the month ended March 31, 2017

Consulting Fees		48,000.00
Less: Expenses		
Commission Expense	7,500.00	
Salaries Expense	18,000.00	
Travel & Entertainment	3,975.00	
Advertising Expense	1,147.50	
Utilities Expense	1,072.50	31,695.00
Net Income		16,305.00

As indicated above, there is net income because revenues are greater than expenses. Also, as earlier mentioned, we need the net income or loss figure in the preparation of the statement of changes in equity. As the statement of changes in equity involves the increases and decreases of the equity account, we only need the income and withdrawal figures to arrive at ending capital balance. This is shown below:

ED GO
Statement of Changes in Equity
for the month ended March 31, 2017

Ed, Capital, beginning	75,000.00
Add: Net Income	16,305.00
Total	91,305.00
Less: Ed, Withdrawal	4,248.00
Ed, Capital, end	87,057.00

Income increases the capital account; thus, it is added to the capital beginning. Withdrawal, or drawing, on the other hand, decreases the capital, so it is deducted to arrive at capital balance end. The capital balance end will now be extended to the capital section of the balance sheet as illustrated in the next page:

ED GO

Balance Sheet

as of March 31, 2017

ASSETS		LIABILITIES	
Current Assets			
Cash	52,767.00	Accounts Payable	6,750.00
Accounts Receivable	19,410.00	Total Liabilities	6,750.00
Office Supplies	525.00		
Prepaid Insurance	6,600.00	CAPITAL	
Prepaid Rent	6,000.00		
Total Current Assets	85,302.00	Ed, Capital	87,057.00
Non-current Assets			
Office Equipment	8,505.00		
TOTAL ASSETS	93,807.00	**TOTAL LIABILITIES AND CAPITAL**	93,807.00

The above format of the balance sheet is called the account form. This is so because the balance sheet looks like a ledger account where the assets which normally have debit balances are presented in the left side, while liabilities and capital which normally have credit balances are presented in the right side.

An alternative format is presented in the next page. This is what is referred to as the report form.

ED GO
Balance Sheet
as of March 31, 2017

ASSETS

Current Assets	
Cash	52,767.00
Accounts Receivable	19,410.00
Office Supplies	525.00
Prepaid Insurance	6,600.00
Prepaid Rent	6,000.00
Total Current Assets	85,302.00
Non-current Assets	
Office Equipment	8,505.00
TOTAL ASSETS	93,807.00

LIABILITIES

Accounts Payable	6,750.00
Total Liabilities	6,750.00

CAPITAL

Ed, Capital	87,057.00
TOTAL LIABILITIES AND CAPITAL	93,807.00

As indicated in the previous pages, the preparation of financial statements is a relatively easy exercise. Financial statements are prepared based on the results of the ledger accounts through the preparation of the trial balance. Revenue and expense accounts constitute the income statement.

Any changes in the capital account, including withdrawals and income/loss are added to the beginning capital balance to prepare the statement of changes in equity. Note that income is added to capital while net loss and withdrawals are deducted from beginning capital balance to arrive at ending capital balance.

Assets, liabilities, and capital (the ending balance from the Statement of Changes in Equity) are the ones reported in the Balance Sheet or Statement of Financial Position.

Other Notes: Adjusting and Closing Entries

It has to be noted that the accounting cycle has two other activities that are not discussed in this book. These are the preparation of adjusting entries and closing entries. Adjusting entries are prepared to ensure that revenues reflected in the financial statements are earned and expenses are incurred at the end of the accounting period. For example, when a business records supplies expense every time a purchase of supplies was made, an inventory of unused supplies at the end of an accounting period can be done. If there are unused supplies, the unused portion of the supplies expense needs to be recognized and the supplies expense needs to be adjusted, to properly reflect this situation. Adjusting entries are not covered in this book.

Closing entries on the other hand are prepared at the end of an accounting period, normally at the end of the year, to transfer the values of nominal accounts (revenues and expenses, including drawing) to real accounts (assets, liabilities, and capital). The process of preparing closing entries involve closing the revenue, expense, and drawing accounts to the capital account either in one single entry or three different entries. A post-closing trial balance is then made to show the remaining balances for all real accounts.

An example is provided below based on Ed Go's financial statements:

   a. To close revenue against capital, the entry would be to simply debit revenues (Consulting Fees) and credit the capital account:

Consulting Fees	48,000.00	
Ed, Capital		48,000.00

   b. To close expense accounts against capital, the entry would be to debit the capital account and credit all expense accounts

Ed, Capital	31,695.00	
Commission Expense		7,500.00
Salary Expense		18,000.00
Travel and Entertainment		3,975.00
Advertising		1,147.50
Utilities		1,072.50

   c. To close drawing against capital, the entry is to debit capital and credit the drawing account

Ed, Capital	4,248.00	
Ed, Drawing		4,248.00

These entries are then posted in the ledger, after which a post-closing trial balance can then be made. See below:

ED GO
Post-Closing Trial Balance
March 31, 2017

ACCOUNT TITLES	Debit	Credit
Cash	52,767.00	
Accounts Receivable	19,410.00	
Office Supplies	525.00	
Prepaid Insurance	6,600.00	
Prepaid Rent	6,000.00	
Office Equipment	8,505.00	
Accounts Payable		6,750.00
Ed, Capital		87,057.00
	93,807.00	93,807.00

Constructively, after the preparation of closing entries, all revenue, expense, and drawing accounts are reduced to zero. These three accounts are called nominal accounts because their balances pertain only to a specific accounting period and are not carried over to the next. Real accounts (assets, liabilities, and capital) are accounts whose balances are carried over from one accounting period to another.

End of Chapter Activities

Exercise 6.1

Name:	Course &year:	Date:
Subject:	Time:	Score:

Discussion Questions. Individually, or as a group, answer the following questions:

1. Why are income statements dated "for the period" while balance sheets are dated "as of a given period of time"?

2. In what way/ways can the balance sheet tell us of the financial condition of an enterprise as of a given period of time?

3. How is the income statement able to tell us the results of operations of a business?

4. What is the objective of each of the financial statements (income, financial position, changes in equity, cash flows)? How are the objectives of each related? Please explain.

5. Why do you think financial statements are important to businessmen?

Exercise 6.2

Name:	Course &year:	Date:
Subject:	Time:	Score:

True or False. Evaluate the following statements. Write on the blank provided before each item T if the statement is TRUE and F if FALSE.

______ 1. The financial position is to the balance sheet as the financial results are to the income statement.

______2. The trial balance when balanced indicates 100% accuracy in recording transactions.

______3. The Income Statement is dated covering a period of time, while the balance sheet is dated for specific time.

______4. The statement of changes in equity shows the revenues and expenses of the business.

______5. The trial balance is one of the basic financial statements.

______6. If revenue is greater than expense, the income statement shows a net income figure.

______7. To be able to prepare the statement of changes in equity, one needs to prepare the income statement first.

______8. The balance sheet shows the financial position of the business as of a given period of time.

______9. Owner's drawing is an essential component of the income statement.

______10. Statement of changes in equity needs to be prepared first before the income statement.

______11. Revenue and expenses are shown in the balance sheet.

______12. Cash inflows and outflows are presented in the cash flow statement.

______13. Balance sheet is the same as Statement of Results of Operation.

______14. Assets in the balance sheet are arranged according to order of liquidity.

______15. There are figures that are shown in the income statement that are carried forward to the balance sheet.

______16. Asset is a real account.

______17. Adjusting entries are prepared to close balances of nominal accounts to real accounts.

______18. Expense is a nominal account.

______19. To ensure that account balances reflect all earned revenue and incurred expense, closing entries are made.

______20. In a post-closing trial balance, the balance of expense accounts is reduced to zero, and are thus not reflected in the report.

Exercise 6.3

Name:	Course &year:	Date:
Subject:	Time:	Score:

Matching Type. Match items in column A with column B. Write the letter of your answer on the blanks provided.

Column A

__________ 1 balance sheet
__________ 2 assets
__________ 3 A = L + C
__________ 4 additional investment
__________ 5 excess of revenue over expense
__________ 6 trial balance
__________ 7 income statement
__________ 8 liabilities
__________ 9 liquidation
__________ 10 R-E=NI/NL
__________ 11 trial balance of balances
__________ 12 excess of expenses over revenues
__________ 13 changes in equity
__________ 14 liquidity
__________ 15 account format

Column B

A net loss
B results of operations
C economic resources
D cash
E balance sheet
F summary of open ledger accounts
G increases capital
H presents balance sheet like a T-account
I financial position
J order of liabilities
K cash flows
L economic obligations
M receipts
N changes in the capital account
O net income
P order of assets
Q income statement
R shows only the balances of each account
S expenses

Exercise 6.4

Name:	Course &year:	Date:
Subject:	Time:	Score:

Problem Solving 1
(Preparation of Financial Statements from Ledger Balances)

Based on the accounts listed below belonging to Allied Legal Services owned by Atty.
Co, prepare

    a. Trial balance
    b. Income statement
    c. Statement of changes in equity
    d. Balance sheet

Interest Expense – P100; Cash – P16,060; Accounts Payable – P3,200; Accounts
Receivable – P12,760; Supplies Expense – P500; Office Furniture – P3,880; Interest
Payable – P500; Co, Capital – P38,000; Office Equipment – 13,200; Salaries and Wages
– P3,000; Legal Fees Income – P14,800; Utilities Expense – P1,000; Rent Expense –
P2,000; Co, Drawing – P2,000; Taxes and Licenses – P2,000

The above transactions happened in May 2017.

Exercise 6.5

Name:	Course &year:	Date:
Subject:	Time:	Score:

Problem Solving 2
Prepare the financial statements based on ledger figures presented below:

CASH — 001

Date		Particulars	F	Amount						Date		Particulars	F	Amount					
10	1	Investment	j-1	2	0	0	0	0	00	10	5	Supplies	j-1			5	0	0	00
	16	Collection	j-2		4	0	0		00		15	Furniture	j-1		9	0	0	0	00
	18	Service income	j-2	1	0	0	0		00		25	Drawing	j-2		4	0	0		00
	30	Investment	j-2	1	0	0	0		00					9	9	0	0		00
				2	2	4	0	0	00										
		12,500 bal																	

ACCOUNTS RECEIVABLE — 002

Date		Particulars	F	Amount					Date		Particulars	F	Amount				
10	7	Income	j-1		7	5	0	00	10	16	Collection	j-2		6	0	0	00
		350 bal															

SUPPLIES — 003

Date		Particulars	F	Amount					Date		Particulars	F	Amount				
10	5	Purchase	j-1		5	0	0	00									
		500 bal															

EQUIPMENT — 004

Date		Particulars	F	Amount						Date		Particulars	F	Amount				
10	1	Investment	j-1		5	0	0	0	00									
	10	Purchase	j-1		3	0	0	0	00									
		8000 bal																

OFFICE FURNITURE — 005

Date		Particulars	F	Amount						Date		Particulars	F	Amount				
10	15	Purchase	j-1		9	0	0	0	00									
		9000 bal																

ACCOUNTS PAYABLE — 006

Date		Particulars	F	Amount						Date		Particulars	F	Amount				
										10	10	Equipment	j-1		3	0	0	0	00

E. POL. CAPITAL											Date		Particulars	F	Amount							007
Date		Particulars	F	Amount							Date		Particulars	F	Amount							
											10	1	Investment	j-1			2	5	0	0	0	00
												30	Investment	j-2				1	0	0	0	00
													26000 bal									

E. POL, WITHDRAWAL																						008
Date		Particulars	F	Amount							Date		Particulars	F	Amount							
10	25	Cash drawing					4	0	0	00												

SERVICE INCOME																						009
Date		Particulars	F	Amount							Date		Particulars	F	Amount							
											10	7	Cash income	j-1					7	5	0	00
												18	Cash income	j-2				1	0	0	0	00
													1750 bal									

These transactions happened in October 2017.

Exercise 6.6

Name:	Course &year:	Date:
Subject:	Time:	Score:

Problem Solving 3

Prepare the financial statements based on the trial balance below:

From the trial balance presented below, prepare the financial statements of Labada Mo, Labado Ko.

Labada Mo, Labada Ko			
Trial Balance			
December 31, 2018			
Account Titles	*Debit*		*Credit*
Cash	178,900.00		
Accounts Receivable	17,600.00		
Notes Receivable	5,000.00		
Building	1,000,000.00		
Accounts Payable			11,400.00
Washer, Capital			1,200,000.00
Washer, Drawing	12,000.00		
Service Income			54,000.00
Permits and Licenses	12,000.00		
Laundry Supplies Expense	16,400.00		
Light and Water	5,000.00		
Salaries	18,500.00		
Balances	**1,265,400.00**		**1,265,400.00**

Exercise 6.7

Name:	Course &year:	Date:
Subject:	Time:	Score:

Problem Solving 4

Prepare the financial statements based on the trial balance presented below:

HOLY NAMES FUNERAL HOMES		
Trial Balance		
12/31/2008		
Account Titles	Debit	Credit
Cash	249,500.00	
Accounts Receivable	75,600.00	
Supplies	22,575.00	
Delivery Equipment	549,788.00	
Service Equipment	22,450.00	
Accounts Payable		35,478.00
Loans Payable		300,000.00
Banban, Capital		500,000.00
Banban, Drawing	12,500.00	
Service Income		129,586.00
Other Income		16,665.00
Salaries and Wages	32,500.00	
Telephone	567.00	
Light and Water	2,750.00	
Fuel and Lubricants	13,499.00	
TOTALS	981,729.00	981,729.00

Exercise 6.8

Name:	Course &year:	Date:
Subject:	Time:	Score:

Closing entries and Post-Closing Trial Balance

Prepare the closing entries and post-closing trial balance based on the information below:

HOLY NAMES FUNERAL HOMES		
Trial Balance		
12/31/2008		
Account Titles	Debit	Credit
Cash	249,500.00	
Accounts Receivable	75,600.00	
Supplies	22,575.00	
Delivery Equipment	549,788.00	
Service Equipment	22,450.00	
Accounts Payable		35,478.00
Loans Payable		300,000.00
Banban, Capital		500,000.00
Banban, Drawing	12,500.00	
Service Income		129,586.00
Other Income		16,665.00
Salaries and Wages	32,500.00	
Telephone	567.00	
Light and Water	2,750.00	
Fuel and Lubricants	13,499.00	
TOTALS	981,729.00	981,729.00

Exercise 6.9

Name:	Course &year:	Date:
Subject:	Time:	Score:

Comprehensive Problem Solving 1

Prepare the financial statements based on the following transactions.

Imang Aerobics Studio conducts aerobics classes. Presented below are transactions during its first month of operations, January 2018.:

Jan	2	Made initial investment of cash, P500,000
	2	Bought aerobics equipment for cash, P300,000
	3	Received loan proceeds from bank, P200,000
	4	Paid rent for the month, P15,000
	5	Paid supplier of complimentary T-shirts given to early enrollees as an advertising promotion, P7,500
	6	Received cash from walk-in clients, P10,000
	7	Billed clients for January class program, P25,000. Clients are expected to pay between January to February 2018
	8	Collected P15,000 from clients on account
	15	Paid salaries of aerobics aides, P5,000
	18	Imang withdrew P2,000 for personal use
	19	Paid P35,000 for sound system equipment
	28	Paid P2,000 for interest of bank loan availed of on January 3
	30	Paid P3,000 for January light and water

Use the following account titles:

01 Cash
02 Accounts Receivable
03 Studio Equipment
04 Loans Payable
05 Imang, Capital
06 Imang, Withdrawal
07 Service Income
08 Advertising Expense
09 Interest Expense
10 Rent Expense
11 Salaries Expense
12 Utilities Expense

Exercise 6.10

Name:	Course &year:	Date:
Subject:	Time:	Score:

Comprehensive Problem Solving 2

Prepare financial statements based on the following transactions:

Ms. ChrisJul owns a self-service laundry shop. She started the business in January and the following business transactions occurred during the month. The laundry shop operates on a cash basis.

Jan	1	ChrisJul invested the following:

        Washing Machine + Dryer   P450,000
        Detergent and Fabric Softener   20,000
        Tables and Chairs   80,000
        Money   50,000

- 2   Received P3,200 from various customers for laundry services
- 3   Received P2,900 from various customers for laundry services
- 5   Received P1,800 from various customers for laundry services
- 7   Paid 2,400 salaries of workers for the week
- 8   Bought additional dryer on account for P40,000
- 12   Received cash of P3,200.00 from various customers
- 14   Paid 60% of account on January 8
- 18   Received cash from various customers for services
- 22   ChrisJul withdrew P5,000 cash from the business
- 24   Paid light and water bill, P4,600
- 30   Paid salaries of workers for 3 weeks P8,600

The following account titles should be used.

Cash	Accounts Payable
Laundry Supplies	ChrisJul, Capital
Laundry Equipment	ChrisJul, Withdrawal
Shop Furniture	Service Income
Office Furniture	Light and Water
	Salaries Expense

Chapter 7. Analyzing Financial Statements

At the end of the chapter the student is expected to:
a. Know and understand the process of analyzing financial statements.
b. Learn basic skills in analyzing the financial statements.
c. Identify the different tools used in analyzing the financial statements.
d. Appreciate the importance of analyzing the financial statements.
e. Articulate the importance of financial analysis in making financial decisions.

Given the fact that in the previous chapter we have already prepared the basic financial statement, we might say that we are now able to complete the discussion of the accounting process. However, this is not the case. As contemplated in the definition, accounting desires that users make an informed decision. Thus, it is not only important for us to know how to prepare financial statements or read them, it is critically important to know how to make use of the financial information we can derive from financial statements.

We go back again to the diagram below, presented in every beginning of the last chapters. In the immediately preceding chapter, we discussed the process by which financial statements are prepared. This is the summarizing phase in accounting. In this case, we have already covered all phases of accounting except the last one - interpreting. In this chapter, we discuss how this phase is very useful not only in financial management, but also in business management.

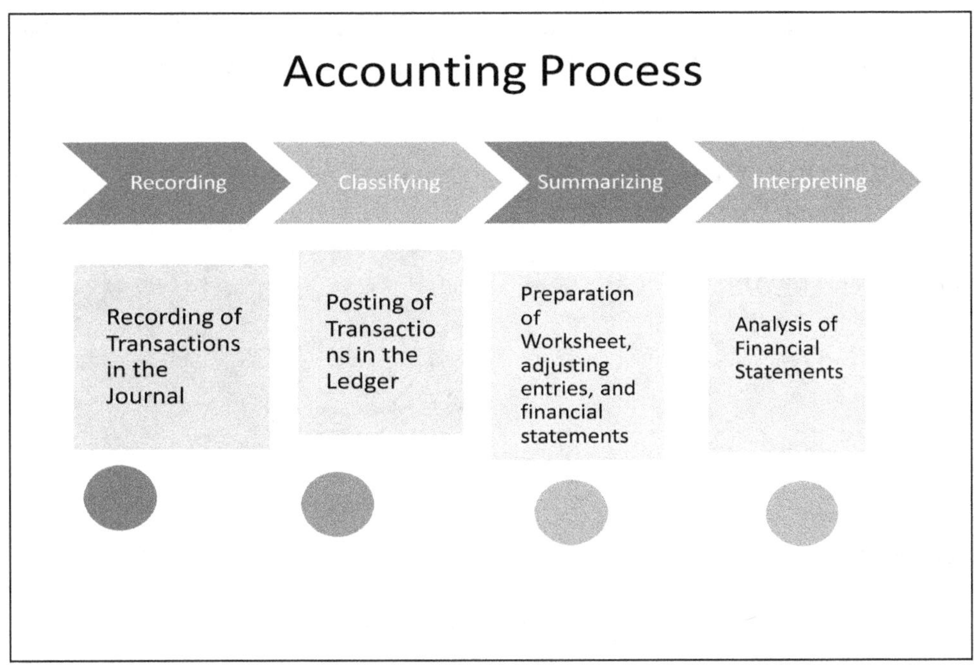

Finding Meaning in the Financial Statement Figures

What if we have prepared a financial statement, is this already useful for purposing of effectively managing a business? Obviously, the answer is no. The financial statements, though considered an end-product in the financial accounting process, are tools in financial management, not ends in themselves. The succeeding step, the utilization of financial information in making informed decisions is equally critical. Thus, it is important to know how we can interpret financial information, how we will be able to analyze it to find value in it and use it in managing our business.

Let us take for example, a particular financial statement balance indicated in the box below:

The above is a financial statement account with a corresponding amount taken out from the balance sheet. By just looking at it, we can have several interpretations:

a. The business has cash.
b. The cash that the business has amounts to P112,250.00.

But we do not get more information from this than the ones mentioned in item a and b. We will not know if cash is enough. We also wouldn't know if the cash balance is good for the business or not. Moreover, we cannot even say if there is a need for us to raise more cash –a decisional aspect in business – and how we will be able to do it. Looking at an account and its balance in the financial statement does not give us very important information.

Let us say for example, we have the financial statement on the next page:

ED GO

Income Statement

for the month ended March 31, 2018

Consulting Fees		48,000.00
Less: Expenses		
Commission Expense	7,500.00	
Salaries Expense	18,000.00	
Travel & Entertainment	3,975.00	
Advertising Expense	1,147.50	
Utilities Expense	1,072.50	31,695.00
Net Income		16,305.00

By looking at the income statement above, we can say several things

a. There are more revenues than expenses, thus resulting to net income.
b. That net income of the business is P16,305.
c. The highest expense is salaries with the amount of P18,000.
d. The lowest expense is utilities with the amount of P1,072.50.

These are just several things that we may be able to see from the above statement. Looking at it deeper, we can say several other observations. For example:

a. If we increase one peso more of revenue, assuming expense does not change, net income will increase in the same amount. This means that revenue maximization (having more sales of services) will have a positive effect in net income (meaning, income will increase).
b. If we decrease one peso in the expense side, assuming revenues do not change, net income will also increase in the same amount. This means that expense minimization (decreasing or controlling expenses) will have a positive effect on net income (meaning net income will increase).

These are just a few of the things that we can say of the income statement we have just seen. However, we can do more interpretations of the financial statements if we use several tools.

In this chapter, we will learn of at least four tools in analysing financial statements:

a. Vertical analysis or translating the financial statement to what we refer to as common-size financial statements.
b. Horizontal analysis, or oftentimes called period analysis or trending
c. Ratio analysis, done by establishing relationships between accounts and amounts in the financial statements

Vertical Analysis

Imagine a vertical line – a line that starts from an upper point to a lower point. If we say vertical analysis, it means that we are analysing an account in the lower or upper part of the financial statement in relation to the other accounts in the financial statements. This is called vertical analysis because the relationships that are analysed are within a financial statement, thus, vertically.

The most common way of conducting a vertical analysis is to convert the financial statement into what is referred to as common-size financial statement. A common size financial statement is one wherein the values are expressed in percentages than in their absolute amounts (Kieso et al 2016). In this case, all figures within the financial statement are converted into percentages of a single denominator. In the case of the income statement, the denominator is usually the total revenues while in the balance sheet, the usual denominator used is total assets.

If for example we use the income statement of Ed Go above, we will be able to get the common size financial statement by dividing each item in the income statement with the denominator P48,000.00. We show the results below:

ED GO
Income Statement
for the month ended March 31, 2018

Consulting Fees		100%
Less: Expenses		
Commission Expense	16%	
Salaries Expense	38%	
Travel & Entertainment	8%	
Advertising Expense	2%	
Utilities Expense	2%	66%
Net Income		34%

As can be seen above, all figures of the income statement are translated into percentages with consulting fees expressed in 100%. This is so because the total revenues, represented here by consulting fees, is the preferred denominator. Based on this common—size financial statement, we can have more interpretations than the ones already mentioned above. These interpretations are shown on the next page:

a. For every peso of consulting fees we generate, we earn 0.34 centavos, or 34%. In this case, the business is considered generally profitable because if money is deposited in the bank, we will only roughly earn between 2% per annum (for savings deposit) to 9% (for time deposits).
b. We spend more on salaries (38%) than on anything else. This is expected because our major product is service, thus, our major expense is on human resource.
c. Advertising expense is more or less equal to utilities expense.

While (b) and (c) above can be deduced without even conducting vertical analysis, the vertical analysis is still important, especially if we would like to compare the performance of one business with another. We cannot compare two businesses using absolute figures. A more meaningful comparison will be done if we compare relative figures by using comparative financial statements.

We illustrate this point below:

Income Statement
for the month ended March 31, 2018

	ED GO		MAR YU	
Consulting Fees		48,000.00		56,000.00
Less: Expenses				
Commission Expense	7,500.00		4,500.00	
Salaries Expense	18,000.00		22,600.00	
Travel & Entertainment	3,975.00		8,567.00	
Advertising Expense	1,147.50		1,123.00	
Utilities Expense	1,072.50	31,695.00	1,750.00	38,540.00
Net Income		16,305.00		17,460.00

Comparing the income statements of Ed Go and Mar Yu above, we may be able to say that Mar Yu performs better for several reasons:

a. Mar Yu has a bigger amount of income
b. Mar Yu has a bigger amount of net income.

However, this may not be the case when we compare percentages with absolute figures as indicated on the next page:

Income Statement for the month ended March 31, 2009	ED GO		MAR YU	
Consulting Fees		100%		100%
Less: Expenses				
Commission Expense	16%		8%	
Salaries Expense	38%		40%	
Travel & Entertainment	8%		15%	
Advertising Expense	2%		2%	
Utilities Expense	2%	66%	3%	69%
Net Income		34%		31%

Our interpretations based on absolute figures of the income statement become erroneous when we will use common size financial statements as a basis for comparison. For example,

a. It is not true that Mar Yu is doing better. While it might be correct to say that Mar Yu generated more consulting fees than Ed Go, however, Ed Go was more prudent in his expenses.
b. In absolute figures, Mar Yu may have shown more income than Ed Go. However, Mar Yu earned less for every peso of consulting revenue it generated. Ed Go earned 34 cents for every peso of consulting fees that it generated while Mar Yu only had 31 cents.
c. While in all other expenses, Ed Go is more cost effective, it spent more commission expense than Mar Yu. It spent twice as much as Mar Yu spent. This should be investigated.

As we have indicated above, vertical analysis is helpful in conducting more meaningful comparisons.

Vertical may also be done with the balance sheet. We present the example on the next page.

ED GO
Balance Sheet
as of March 31, 2018

ASSETS		LIABILITIES	
Current Assets			
Cash	56%	Accounts Payable	7%
Accounts Receivable	21%	Total Liabilities	7%
Office Supplies	1%		
Prepaid Insurance	7%	CAPITAL	
Prepaid Rent	6%		
Total Current Assets	91%	Ed, Capital	93%
Non-current Assets			
Office Equipment	9%		
TOTAL ASSETS	100%	TOTAL LIABILITIES AND CAPITAL	100%

Using the above data, we can say several things:

a. Majority (56%) of the total assets of the business is cash. This means that cash is readily available for business operations.
b. The business has very small amount of liabilities. This means that the business is not tied up with paying external obligations.
c. Most of the business assets are current.

What other observations can you make based on the above data?

Horizontal Analysis

A horizontal analysis is a process of comparing financial statements across periods, thus, the name horizontal (Edmonds et al 2014). In other books, this is called trending, which means, we establish a trend of accounts and amounts in the financial statements to observe some generalizations. We will illustrate this point in the next page using the business of Ed Go.

Income Statement

Comparative Income Statement

for the years 2016 – 2018

	2016	2017	2018
Consulting Fees	345,000.00	325,000.00	387,500.00
Less: Expenses			
Commission Expense	31,050.00	29,250.00	34,875.00
Salaries Expense	189,540.00	191,651.00	199,450.00
Travel & Entertainment	12,456.00	15,456.00	17,456.00
Advertising Expense	35,245.00	45,123.00	32,155.00
Utilities Expense	12,156.00	13,111.00	13,879.00
Total Expenses	280,447.00	294,591.00	297,815.00
Net Income	64,553.00	30,409.00	89,685.00

The above comparative statements will give us several interpretations. For example, we can say that net income is dependent on the consulting revenues generated. We can also say that the business performed poorly in 2017 but was able to recover in 2018. Also, we can observe that we spent more on advertising in 2017 than in any other year. These are several of the interpretations we can see using the above comparative financial statement. What else can you observe based on the above figures?

When we conduct horizontal analysis, we compare figures of the current period with those of the previous years, thereby creating a trendline. We can do this by creating a line graph using absolute figures. This is easy to do using a spreadsheet software where graphs can be generated automatically.

This is illustrated in the next page:

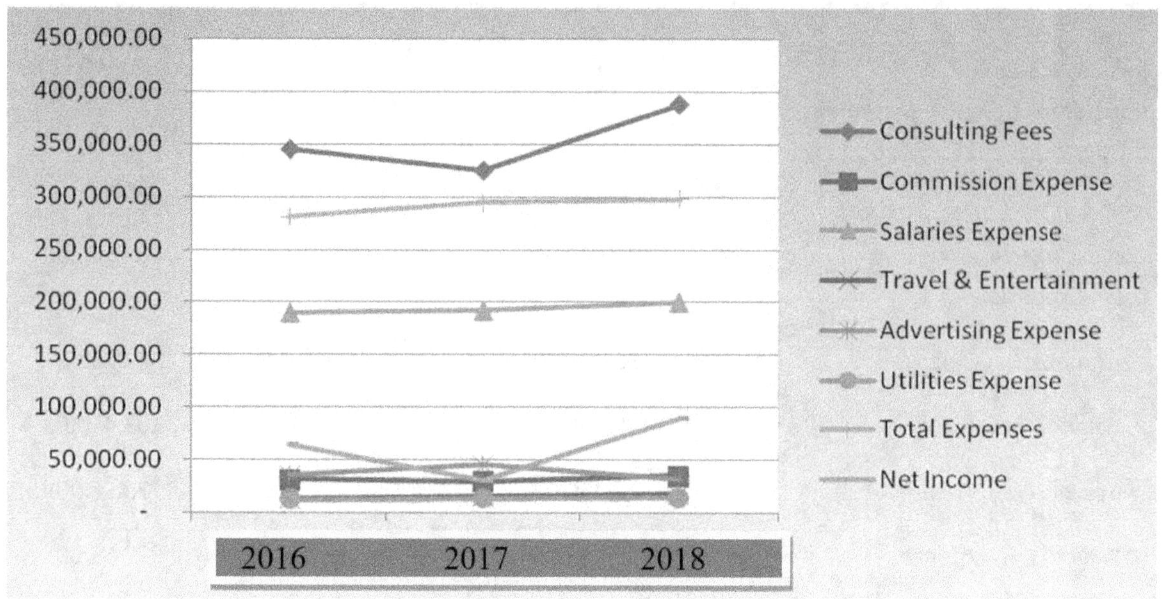

As can be observed above, there are some expenses which are relatively constant (commission) while others have erratic patterns (advertising). Consulting fees, as earlier observed dipped in 2017 but recovered in 2018 with an amount greater than 2016. Doing these comparisons are important for decision-making purposes.

Horizontal analysis, however, is done using percentages, by comparing one year's balances with that of the previous. What will be computed is percent of change from the previous year and is computed using the following formula:

Percent of Change =   Current year's amount – previous year's amount
                                      Previous year's amount

In this case, the previous year is considered the base year. If the answer is positive, this means that there is an increase in the amount. If the answer is negative, on the other hand, this indicates a decrease in the amount.

The change can either be favourable or unfavourable depending on the figures compared. In brief, the following can be said.

a. A positive percent of change, when this is a revenue account, is considered favourable because revenue increased in the current period, as compared the previous year. Conversely, if a revenue account has a negative percent of change, this is unfavourable because revenue decreased in the current period as compared the previous year.

b. A positive percent of change for expense accounts is considered unfavourable because expenses increased in the current period, as compared the previous year. Conversely, a negative percent of change for expense accounts is favourable because expenses decreased in the current period as compared the previous year.

c. A positive percent of change for asset accounts can be considered favourable, especially if this is caused by either investment or income utilized for asset acquisitions.

d. A positive percent of change for liability accounts is considered unfavourable because this means that the business incurred more liabilities in the current period as compared the previous year.

These are just some of the few things we can explain regarding positive and negative percent of change. We test this proposition below:

ED GO

Income Statement

Comparative Income Statement

for the years 2017 – 2018

	2017	2018
Consulting Fees	-6%	19%
Less: Expenses		
Commission Expense	-6%	19%
Salaries Expense	1%	4%
Travel & Entertainment	24%	13%
Advertising Expense	28%	-29%
Utilities Expense	8%	6%
Total Expenses	55%	13%
Net Income	-61%	6%

The above computation is based on the same figures as the one indicated in the immediately preceding table and graph. It can be observed that there are no figures for 2016 because this was the comparison year without any preceding year in the given problem. We can mention several things here by just looking at the table above.

a. There is a significant drop in revenues from consulting fees between 2016 and 2017 but was later recovered by 2010 figures.

b. Commission expense has a direct relationship with consulting fees revenue. The amount, in this case, might be fixed at a certain percentage from the total consulting fees revenue generated during the year.

c. There was a very big decrease in net income between 2016 and 2017. The amount of decrease was not recovered by the succeeding year, with potential repercussions on the company in terms of investor trust and confidence.

Above are just a few of the things that we may be able to say about the organizational financial statements. What else do you think can be interpreted from the horizontal analysis above?

Ratio Analysis

Now we turn to the last cluster of analysis tools that we will be learning in this chapter – ratio analysis.   Ratio analysis is conducted by establishing plausible relationships between accounts and amounts in the financial statements. These accounts selected for ratio analysis normally have predictable relationships. For example, net income can be compared against equity – with the assumption that a businessman invests in a venture because he or she expects a return on his/her every peso of investment. There are many analysis tools that we can use for ratio analysis, however, we will only focus on a few things in this chapter.

First, we will learn about ratios that can be studied using the balance sheet. We present again below the balance sheet of ED GO as of March 31, 2018.

ED GO
Balance Sheet
as of March 31, 2018

ASSETS		LIABILITIES	
Current Assets			
Cash	52,767.00	Accounts Payable	6,750.00
Accounts Receivable	19,410.00	Total Liabilities	6,750.00
Office Supplies	525.00		
Prepaid Insurance	6,600.00	CAPITAL	
Prepaid Rent	6,000.00		
Total Current Assets	85,302.00	Ed, Capital	87,057.00
Non-current Assets			
Office Equipment	8,505.00		
TOTAL ASSETS	93,807.00	TOTAL LIABILITIES AND CAPITAL	93,807.00

<u>Ratio 1: Debt-Equity Ratio</u>

The debt to equity ratio tells us of the capital structure of the business as of a given period of time (Ainsworth and Deines 2016). It tells us whether creditors own more the business than its proprietor. The formula is simple, and we present this below together with the corresponding computation using ED GO's data above.

Formula   <u>Total Liabilities</u>

	Total Capital
Computation	6,750
	87,057
Answer	7.75%
Implication	This means that the business is financed more by owner's investment than by creditors because the debt is only 7.75% of the equity.

Ratio 2: Debt Ratio

The debt ratio is a slight variation of the debt-equity ratio (Brigham and Houston 2009). It tells us how much of the total equity of the business (creditor's and owner's equity) is provided by creditors.

Formula	Total Liabilities
	Total Equity (Liabilities + Capital)
Computation	6,750
	93,807
Answer	7.19%
Implication	This means that of the total assets by the business, only 7.19% are financed by the creditors.

Ratio 3: Equity Ratio

The equity ratio is a slight variation of the debt-equity ratio. It tells us how much of the total equity of the business (creditor's and owner's equity) is provided by owner's (Larson et al 2005, 689).

Formula	Total Owner's Capital
	Total Equity (Liabilities + Capital)
Computation	87,057
	93,807
Answer	92.8%
Implication	This means that of the total assets by the business, majority (92.8%) are financed by the owners.

If we add the debt ratio and the equity ratio, we will get 100%.

Ratio 4: Current Ratio

The current ratio tells us the state of liquidity of the business by comparing total current assets with current liabilities (Gitman & Zutter 2012). This tests the business' ability to pay its currently maturing obligations – how much current assets are available to pay its current liabilities.

Formula	Current Assets
	Current Liabilities
Computation	85,302
	6,750
Answer	1263.73%
Implication	This means that the business is highly liquid. It has Php12.63 available to pay P1.00 of currently maturing obligation.

Ratio 5: Quick Ratio

The quick ratio, like the current ratio, tells us the state of liquidity of the business by comparing quick assets with current liabilities (Bazley et al 2010). By quick assets we mean cash and cash equivalents, and inventory. This is therefore a stricter test of liquidity than current ratio.

Formula	Quick Assets
	Current Liabilities
Computation	72,177
	6,750
Answer	1069.28%
Implication	This also means that the business is highly liquid. It has Php10.69 quick assets available to pay P1.00 of currently maturing obligation.

In the succeeding ratios, we will use a combination of balance sheet and income statement figures. To facilitate this, we present again the income statement of ED GO.

ED GO
Income Statement
for the month ended March 31, 2018

Consulting Fees		48,000.00
Less: Expenses		
Commission Expense	7,500.00	
Salaries Expense	18,000.00	
Travel & Entertainment	3,975.00	
Advertising Expense	1,147.50	
Utilities Expense	1,072.50	31,695.00
Net Income		16,305.00

Ratio 6: Return on Assets

Return on Assets is a test of profitability (Penman 2010). It tells us how much income is earned for every asset used in the conduct of the business. The higher the return on asset, the better it is for the business. This is shown in the example below:

Formula	Net Income / Total Assets
Computation	16,305 / 93,807
Answer	17.38%
Implication	This means that the business is relatively profitable. For every peso of asset used in operating the business, there is a corresponding 17 cents earned. This is profitable because bank interest rate is currently at 2 to 9%.

Ratio 7: Return on Equity

Return on Equity is also a test of profitability. It tells us how much income is earned for every peso invested by the owner in the business (Ross et al 2008). The higher the return on equity, the more favourable it is for the owner.

Formula	Net Income / Total Owner's Capital
Computation	16,305 / 87,057
Answer	18.73%

Implication
        This means that the business is relatively profitable. For every peso invested by the owner in the business, he earns 18 centavos. As indicated above, this is already profitable because current bank interest rate is between 2 to 9%.

These are just some of the ratios used in the business for analysing status and performance. Ratios 1 to 3 are ratios to analyze capital structure while ratios 4 and 5 tests liquidity of the business, or its ability to pay obligations as they fall due. Finally, ratios 6 and 7 are profitability tests used largely to determine if a business venture is profitable or not.

These are just a few of the tools that we use to analyse financial statements. Vertical analysis shows us the relationships of accounts within the same financial statement while horizontal analysis compares performance across different periods. Finally, ratio analysis shows us that certain relationships between accounts in the financial statements can give us insights into a business' liquidity, profitability, or stability.

End of Chapter Exercises

Exercise 7.1

Name:	Course &year:	Date:
Subject:	Time:	Score:

Discussion Questions. Individually, or in groups, answer the following questions.

1. What is the interpreting phase of accounting? What does this phase intend to accomplish or achieve?

2. In what way will horizontal analysis help businessmen in making decisions for the business?

3. What is the importance of conducting vertical analysis? How useful do you think is it for businessmen?

4. Which among the financial statement analysis tools that you have learned in this chapter is the most useful for businessmen? Why?

Exercise 7.2

Name:	Course &year:	Date:
Subject:	Time:	Score:

Multiple Choice: Select the best answer from the choices given in each item. Encircle of the letter of the answer that corresponds to your choice.

1. Vertical analysis is a financial statement analysis tool that
   a. Tests plausible relationships between accounts and amounts in the financial statements
   b. Relates one item in the financial statement to another, expressing the amount in percentage to that of the base figure
   c. Compares accounts and amounts in one period with those of a prior period
   d. None of these
2. Horizontal analysis is a financial statement analysis tool that
   a. Tests plausible relationships between accounts and amounts in the financial statements
   b. Relates one item in the financial statement to another, expressing the amount in percentage to that of the base figure
   c. Compares accounts and amounts in one period with those of a prior period
   d. None of these
3. Ratio analysis is a financial statement analysis tool that
   a. Tests plausible relationships between accounts and amounts in the financial statements
   b. Relates one item in the financial statement to another, expressing the amount in percentage to that of the base figure
   c. Compares accounts and amounts in one period with those of a prior period
   d. None of these
4. Which among the following results to common-size financial statement?
   a. Vertical analysis
   b. Horizontal analysis
   c. Ratio analysis
   d. None of these
5. Which among the following results to the determination of increase or decrease in amounts?
   a. Vertical analysis
   b. Horizontal analysis
   c. Ratio analysis
   d. None of these
6. Which of the following is a profitability ratio?
   a. Debt ratio
   b. Quick ratio
   c. Equity ratio
   d. Return on assets
7. Which of the following is a ratio that measures liquidity?
   a. debt-equity ratio
   b. Quick ratio
   c. Return on equity
   d. None of these
8. Which of the following ratios measures capital structure?
   a. Debt-equity ratio
   b. Current ratio
   c. Return on equity
   d. Return on assets

9. Which is not a quick asset?
   a. inventory
   b. cash
   c. Receivables
   d. Office supplies
10. Which among the following ratio analysis tools will help us determine the improvements in the financial performance of the business over time?
    a. Horizontal analysis
    b. Ratio analysis
    c. Vertical analysis
    d. None of these

Exercise 7.3

Name:	Course &year:	Date:
Subject:	Time:	Score:

True or False: Evaluate the statements given in each item below. On the blank provided, write T if the statement is True and F if False.

1. In a horizontal analysis, a positive increase is always considered favourable.
2. A large figure in the return on assets in unfavourable to the owner of the business.
3. Debt to equity ratio tells us of the liquidity position of the business.
4. The objective of a vertical analysis is to compare two businesses as of a period.
5. Quick ratio is a test of liquidity.
6. The higher the positive increase in a horizontal analysis, the better it is for revenue accounts.
7. The higher the negative increase in a horizontal analysis, the better it is for liability accounts.
8. A debt ratio of 80% is favourable to the business.
9. A debt-equity ratio of 5% is favourable to the business.
10. Current ratio is the same as quick ratio.
11. A current ratio of 2% is unfavourable to the business.
12. Quick ratio is also a measure of profitability.
13. Common size financial statements are financial statements expressed in percentages.
14. An increasing trend for assets in horizontal analysis is favourable.
15. A decreasing trend for expenses in horizontal analysis is favourable.

Exercise 7.4

Name:	Course &year:	Date:
Subject:	Time:	Score:

Problem Exercise. Vertical Analysis. Prepare a common-size income statement for the following financial statements:

Makisama Enterprises
Income Statement
September 31, 2010

Store Service Revenues		146,750.20
Less: Operating Expenses		
Salaries Expense	34,500.00	
Rent Expense	18,000.00	
Communication	3,395.40	
Advertising	25,000.00	
Light and Water	5,675.80	86,571.20
Net Income		60,179.00

Makisama Enterprises
Balance Sheet
September 31, 2010

ASSETS

Current Assets		
Cash	163,942.00	
Accounts Receivable	35,300.00	
Store Supplies	6,750.00	205,992.00
Non-Current Assets		
Store Equipment	78,500.00	
Store Furniture	135,687.00	214,187.00
TOTAL ASSETS		**420,179.00**
LIABILITIES		
Accounts Payable		50,000.00
Loans Payable		100,000.00
OWNER'S CAPITAL		
Maki, Capital		270,179.00
TOTAL LIABILITIES AND CAPITAL		**420,179.00**

Exercise 7.5

Name:	Course &year:	Date:
Subject:	Time:	Score:

Problem Exercise: Horizontal Analysis. Prepare a horizontal analysis for the following financial statements:

Makisama Enterprises

Balance Sheet

	2016	2017	2018
ASSETS			
Cash	163,942.00	139,350.70	189,505.00
Accounts Receivable	35,300.00	39,300.00	52,600.00
Store Supplies	6,750.00	5,450.00	7,859.00
Store Equipment	78,500.00	62,800.00	50,240.00
Store Furniture	135,687.00	122,118.30	109,906.47
TOTAL ASSETS	420,179.00	369,019.00	410,110.47
LIABILITIES			
Accounts Payable	50,000.00	40,000.00	52,500.00
Loans Payable	100,000.00	80,000.00	60,000.00
OWNER'S CAPITAL			
Maki, Capital	270,179.00	249,019.00	297,610.47
TOTAL LIABILITIES AND CAPITAL	420,179.00	369,019.00	410,110.47

Exercise 7.6

Name:	Course &year:	Date:
Subject:	Time:	Score:

Problem Exercises. Ratio Analysis. Use the following financial statements in solving for the requirements contained in the last paragraph.

Makisama Enterprises
Income Statement
September 31, 2010

Store Service Revenues		146,750.20
Less: Operating Expenses		
Salaries Expense	34,500.00	
Rent Expense	18,000.00	
Communication	3,395.40	
Advertising	25,000.00	
Light and Water	5,675.80	86,571.20
Net Income		60,179.00

Makisama Enterprises
Balance Sheet
September 31, 2010

ASSETS

Current Assets

Cash	163,942.00	
Accounts Receivable	35,300.00	
Store Supplies	6,750.00	205,992.00

Non-Current Assets

Store Equipment	78,500.00	
Store Furniture	135,687.00	214,187.00
TOTAL ASSETS		**420,179.00**

LIABILITIES

Accounts Payable	50,000.00
Loans Payable	100,000.00

OWNER'S CAPITAL

Maki, Capital	270,179.00

TOTAL LIABILITIES AND CAPITAL	**420,179.00**

Compute for the following ratios and explain its meaning.
    a. Quick ratio
    b. Current ratio
    c. Debt ratio
    d. Equity ratio
    e. Debt-equity ratio
    f. Return on assets
    g. Return on equity

Chapter 8. Accounting for Tourism-related Establishments

After the end of the chapter the student is expected to:
  a. Distinguish hotels and other related businesses from other types of businesses in so far as revenues and expenses are concerned.
  b. Apply basic skills in recording transactions specific to hotel and restaurant businesses
  c. Actualize basic analytical skills in interpreting financial statements of resorts and hotels.

In the previous chapters, we have already covered the whole accounting cycle, however, examples were made on the basis of a generalized service-concern business. The reason for doing so is to make the discussions simple and generic so that the knowledge acquired from the previous sessions will become sufficient to equip us with the skills to prepare and more importantly, to understand financial statements.

In this chapter we will focus on how accounting is applied to tourism-related establishments. Tourism-related establishments are chosen as a major item for discussion in this chapter primarily because most students taking this course are taking up tourism-related courses. Secondly, tourism-related establishments are easier to comprehend and the nature of these business, like hotels, agencies, resorts, and restaurants are interesting to analyse and investigate.

The Nature of Tourism-related Establishments

In its simplest form, tourism-related establishments are businesses that offer services to tourists or those that support tourism activities (Cruz 2009). This may range from businesses that offer transport, accommodation, food, to those that offer entertainment, facilitation, and other related services. A car rental company like Avis or Varescon is a tourism-related establishment though it does not only serve tourists. A restaurant also is considered tourism-related though it offers service to the general public. Thus, it has to be noted that most tourism-related establishments do not only serve tourists, though in most cases, they exist to serve the needs for this particular market. It has to be noted that while restaurants offer food, it is considered a service-concern type of business, as indicated earlier in chapter 1 of this book.

It is therefore safe to say that most tourism-related establishments offer services to the public. We can segregate these establishments by the nature of service it offers, as indicated below:

Nature of Service	Examples
Transport	Taxi company, rent-a-car, bus rental, cruise ship
Accommodation	Hotel, resorts, pension house, inn, lodge,
Facilitation	Travel agency, ticketing office, internet booking engine
Food service	Restaurant, fast-food, snack bar, noodle shop
Entertainment	Bar, theatre, adventure camps, floating cottage, museum

However, in this chapter, we will not cover all establishments indicated above. The two areas of interest in this chapter are businesses that offer accommodation and those that offer food service.

Accounting for Hotels and Other Similar Establishments

Hotels offer one major service – accommodation to guests. Hotels may offer other services like foreign currency exchange, minibar, restaurant, spa services, all these are considered auxiliary income sources and are accounted for separately. This is the reason why, we oftentimes see in the income statement of resort the following revenue items:

Rooms
Transient Rooms Sales
Group Rooms Sales
Contract Rooms Sales

Food and Beverage
Restaurant Sales
Minibar Sales
Poolbar Sales

Other Income
Telephone Sales
Gift Shop Sales
Rents and Commissions
Other Sales

We can say that there are at least three major areas where hotels earn income from – these are on rooms, F and B, and other auxiliary sources. It is to be noted however that not all establishments offering accommodation have all these income types. Income sources are entirely dependent on the services provided by the establishment.

Room Sales
Rooms can be sold to walk-in or transient guests. These can also be sold to pre-booked guests who either contract a travel agent to manage their booking for them or self-manage the booking on their own via online transactions.   Rooms can also be sold to groups. Room rates, in this case, will largely differ. Walk-in guests normally pay more than

those pre-booked guests, and much more when compared to those with group bookings, that because of larger transaction volume enjoy discounted rates.

The manner of payment will largely differ. Some guests may pay in cash upon booking, especially when room deposit payment is required. Other guests may pay through credit cards, either upon booking or upon check-in. Still others can pay to their travel agent who in turn will remit payment to the hotel. It is important to note these because journal entry for each type of payment will differ.

Food and Beverage Sales
The F and B of most hotels are treated as a separate department. This involves sales from the restaurant, the mini-bar, the pool bar, among others. Guests may opt to pay, again, through credit card or cash, or they may choose to have their consumption charged against their room bill which they will settle upon check-out. We will deal with F and B later.

Other Income Sources
As earlier indicated, other income sources will depend on the type of services offered by the resort. These other income sources can be any of the following:

a. Store sales – this can be the ministore (basic amenities for sale at the front desk), the gift-shop, or souvenir shop.
b. Communication revenue – this involves sales from guest's use of telephone for local and international calls, internet, facsimile services
c. Rental – this may involve rental of hotel equipment and facilities like computer, bicycle, pool, gym equipment, jetski, kayak
d. Service Income – this may come from offering different services as spa, haircut, manicure, among others
e. Commission – revenue normally from other businesses that the hotel recommends for usual services like car rental, massage clinic, when it does not provide these services on its own.

Sample Problem:

In the sample problem below, we highlight only those items that will reveal the intricacies of hotels.

List of Transactions:

August

1   Two guests, X and Y arrived without booking, occupied two separate rooms. The front office swiped the cards of the guests but will only collect payment after checking out.

2   Guest Q arrived with a travel voucher from an Agent Z. He would stay for 2 nights.

3   Guest A arrived and occupied one room. He made a room deposit of P1,200

| 4 | | The 2 guests on August 1 checked out and paid their accounts in full. They used two motorbikes at P1,000 per day rental on August 2. Total restaurant bill was P2,220. Guest X paid for the total bill. |
| 5 | | Guest A checked out. No other hotel bills. |

Room rate is P1,200, with 10% off on contracted or travel agent rates.

Answers with Explanations:

August 1 Transactions

Date		Particulars	Debit	Credit
8	1	Accounts Receivable – X	1200	
		Accounts Receivable – Y	1200	
		Room Revenue		2400
		Room sales for the period		

We record accounts receivable because upon check in, guests are already liable to pay for at least one day of room use.

August 2 Transactions

We record charges on a daily basis, in such a way that on August 2, we record the following journal entry.

Date		Particulars	Debit	Credit
8	2	Accounts Receivable – X	1200	
		Accounts Receivable – Y	1200	
		Room Revenue		2400
		Room sales for the period		

The journal entry above is to accumulate room charges to both X and Y in as much as they have not checked out yet. The reason why we do not record the receivable for the whole time of their stay because we may not know when they will decide to check out.

There is another transaction on August 2 and we need to record it as below:

Date		Particulars	Debit	Credit
8	2	Accounts Receivable – Agent Z	2160	
		Commission Expense	240	
		Room Revenue		2400
		Room sales for the period		

As can be seen above, upon the guest's check in, we did not record a receivable from Q, but from his agent. This is because Q has already paid Agent Z and what we will do in this case is to bill Agent Z. Notice also that the receivable we record is already the 2 nights instead of only 1 as indicated for walk-in guests. This is because agent room sales are already prepaid, and thus, the guest will surely stay for the number of nights indicated in the room voucher. Finally, the amount we record as receivable from Agent Z is already net of his commission with the 240 balancing figure charged against commission expense. It is allowed, however, that we will record the full amount of the receivable (at P2400) and will only record the commission expense upon the receipt of payment from Z. In any case, the financial statement effect is still the same.

August 3 Transactions

Because Guest X and Y have not yet checked out, we record one-night charge more as receivable from them as shown below:

Date		Particulars	Debit	Credit
8	3	Accounts Receivable – X	1200	
		Accounts Receivable – Y	1200	
		Room Revenue		2400
		Room sales for the period		

As Guest A arrived and took one room, we will also record his payment as follows:

Date		Particulars	Debit	Credit
8	3	Cash	1200	
		Room Revenue		1200
		Room sales for the period		

It is customary for resort front desk to either ask for credit cards upon check in for verification purposes or a full one-night deposit. In the transaction above, Guest A deposited full amount instead of giving out his credit card.

August 4 Transactions

On this date, two guests that arrived in August 1 checked out. In this case, it is important to compute their final bill. In most cases, a hotel bill looks this way.

BO HOTEL
Statement of Account

Name of Guest	X and Y		Date of Stay	From	1-Aug
Address	Philippines			To	3-Aug
ID No.	11313/45912		Rate:	Regular	

Date	Particulars	Reference	Amount
1-Aug	Room Charge - X	AR111	1,200.00
	Room Charge - Y	AR111	1,200.00
2-Aug	Room Charge - X	AR231	1,200.00
	Room Charge - Y	AR231	1,200.00
2-Aug	Motorbike Rental	AR456	2,000.00
3-Aug	Room Charge - X	AR581	1,200.00
	Room Charge - Y	AR581	1,200.00
4-Aug	Total F and B bills	SB012	2,220.00
	TOTAL BILL		11,420.00
	Less: Deposit, if any		0
	TOTAL BILL PAYABLE		**11,420.00**

Given the above billing statement, we will be able to prepare the entry upon preparation of official receipt, as follows:

Date		Particulars	Debit	Credit
8	4	Cash	11420	
		Accounts Receivable- X		3600
		Accounts Receivable-Y		3600
		Accounts Receivable – X and Y (bike room charge)		2000
		Accounts Receivable – X and Y (F&B room charge)		2220
		To record payment of hotel and other charges		

We have to take note that the bills for both resort and other services are considered as AR at the time the guest availed of the services. Thus, the entry above is to cancel all receivables that were recorded for X and Y.

Since Guest A did not check out yet, we also need to make the following entry below:

Date		Particulars	Debit	Credit
8	4	Accounts Receivable – A	1200	
		Room Revenue		1200
		Room sales for the period		

Notice that the entry we made is no longer similar to the entry made when A checked in. This is because A already paid for the first night in advance, at the time of check in. For August 4, his second night, he no longer paid his room charge. Presumably, he will settle this upon check out.

<u>August 5 Transactions</u>

On this date, Guest A checked out. We also need to look at his hotel bill as presented below.

Statement of Account

Name of Guest	A		Date of Stay	From	1-Aug
Address	Philippines			To	3-Aug
ID No.	11313/45912		Rate:	Regular	

Date	Particulars	Reference	Amount
3-Aug	Room Charge - A		1,200.00
4-Aug	Room Charge - A	AR 568	1,200.00
	TOTAL BILL		2,400.00
	Less: Deposit, if any	OR 1156	1,200.00
	TOTAL BILL PAYABLE		**1,200.00**

Note that in the above bill, the August 4 room charge is without reference because this was already paid for. The amount of P1200 however, is still indicated for purposes of accounting. Nevertheless, the deposit was deducted to get the total bill payable. Upon A's payment, the journal entry below will appear in the books of accounts:

Date		Particulars	Debit	Credit
8	5	Cash	1200	
		Accounts Receivable – A		1200
		Final settlement of hotel bills.		

Sample Financial Statements of a Hotel

The above illustration of journal entries will then be posted to ledger, going through the same process as the ones elaborated in the previous chapters until a final statement is prepared.

On the next page, we present a sample income statement of a hotel:

BO HOTEL
Profit and Loss Statement
for the period ended December 31, 2017

REVENUES

4100 · Accommodation Income		4,077,780.00
4120 · Ministore Sales		213,566.00
4300 · Service Revenue		15,900.00
4400 · Rental Revenue		23,420.00
4500 · Communications Revenue		15,990.00
4600 · Commission Revenue		23,133.00
GROSS INCOME		4,369,789.00
LESS: OPERATING EXPENSES		
5042 · Staff meals	16,222.22	
5100 · Room Supplies	24,957.00	
5200 · Salaries & Wages	243,529.00	
5400 · Maintenance/Repairs	544,725.77	
5500 · Communication Expense	46,642.82	
5550 · Utilities Expense	199,994.15	
5600 · Office Expenses	45,429.15	
5700 · Front Office Supplies	11,766.33	
5750 · Taxes & Licenses	82,095.66	
5760 · Insurance Expense	40,000.00	
5850 · Promotions & Advertising	96,681.62	
5900 · Contracted Services	138,303.49	
5950 · Commission Expense	404.00	
6000 · Administrative Expenses	62,942.91	
6050 · Service Charge-Credit Cards	17,952.86	1,571,646.99
NET INCOME		**2,798,142.01**

As can be noted above, the format, manner of presentation of income statements is entirely the same as what you have learned in the previous chapter. It goes without saying that the balance sheet also looks entirely the same, as presentation of financial statements and the accounting process do not differ with the type of business.

A condensed balance sheet of the same establishment is presented on the next page:

BO HOTEL
Balance Sheet
for the period ended December 31, 2017

Assets		Liabilities	
Current Assets			
Cash	451,200.00	Accounts Payable	487,599.00
Accounts Receivable	213,333.00	Loans Payable	822,405.00
Supplies Inventory	56,480.00	SSS/PHIC/HDMF Payable	1,250.00
Other Current Assets	14,220.00		
Non-Current Assets			
Room Furniture	1,241,500.00	**Capital**	
Lobby Furniture	245,690.00	Bo, Capital	1,031,169.00
Equipments	120,000.00		
TOTAL ASSETS	**2,342,423.00**	**TOTAL LIABILITIES AND CAPITAL**	**2,342,423.00**

Accounting for Restaurants

Financial statements of restaurants are prepared in the same way as any other form of business and like the one presented above. However, a distinct variation of restaurant accounting is the use of Cost of Sales, also referred to as Food and Beverage Cost. Simply put, Cost of Sales represents the cost of generating restaurant sales (or food and beverage sales). If a business sells rice toppings with choices of beef and chicken, Food Cost represent the cost of chicken, rice, seasoning, spices and thus form part of Cost of Sales. If with the rice toppings, the restaurant sells mango shake, Beverage Cost represents milk, sugar, mango, ice, and ice cream and this forms part of Cost of Sales.

Cost of sales has several components and includes the following:

a. Inventory, beginning – the cost of goods purchased at the start of business or at the beginning of the period.
b. Purchases – this represent the costs of goods purchased during the period.
c. Purchase discounts – deduction from the amount to be paid from goods purchased on account due to prompt payment.
d. Purchase returns – goods purchased but returned to suppliers
e. Freight in – the amount paid for bringing the goods from the supplier to the restaurant
f. Total Cost of Goods Available for sale – computed by adding inventory beginning and net purchases (purchases + freight in – purchase discounts – purchase returns).

g. Inventory, ending – the cost of goods that remain unused at the end of the period.

The Cost of Sales is normally shown in the income statement in the following manner:

Food and Beverage Sales			XXXX
Less: Cost of Sales			
Inventory, beginning		XXX	
Add: Net Purchases			
Purchases	XXX		
Add: Freight In	XXX		
Total	XXX		
Less: Purchase Returns	XXX		
Purchase Discounts	XXX	XXX	
Total Goods Available		XXX	
Less: Inventory, end		XXX	XXX
Gross Profit			
Less: Operating Expenses			
Salaries		XXX	
Rent		XXX	
Utilities		XXX	XXX
NET INCOME			XXX

From the above presentation, we can generate the following formulae:

a. Net Income = Food and Beverage Sales – Cost of Sales – Operating Expenses
b. Cost of Sales = Inventory, beginning + Net Purchases – Inventory, end
c. Net Purchases = Purchases + Freight in – Purchase Returns – Purchase Discounts
d. Total Goods Available = Inventory beginning + Net Purchases

The logic of these formulae is simple.

For example, if we start selling today rice topping with chicken, we need to buy chicken, rice, and other ingredients first. Therefore, because we have not bought anything yet, our inventory, beginning is zero. All the things we purchase, just as long as they form part of the finished product that we sell (chicken rice toppings), this is all considered as purchases. This means that tissue paper for the restaurant tables is not considered part of Cost of Sales; they are referred to as Restaurant Supplies, instead. Then we start cooking. At the end of the day, we count all those ingredients that we have bought that were still unused. This is our inventory end. We deduct from our purchases the inventory end, we get the amount of cost that was used for generating the day's sales. It is useful to note that the ending inventory of one period becomes the beginning inventory of the succeeding period.

For purposes of illustrating how components of the cost of sales are entered in the journal, the problem on the next page is presented:

Sample Transactions

Jan 2 Purchased merchandise on account from Drilon Co., 2/10, n/30, P20,000
3 Paid freight on goods purchased, P750
4 Returned merchandise to Drilon Co. P1,000

Answers

Date		Particulars	Debit	Credit
1	2	*Purchases*	*20000*	
		Accounts Payable		*20000*
		Purchased goods on account		
		#		
	3	*Freight In*	*750*	
		Cash		*750*
		Paid freight of goods purchased		
		#		
	4	*Accounts Payable*	*1000*	
		Purchase Returns		*1000*
		Payment of account		

In the January 2 transaction, we recorded the purchases of the goods while in 3rd January, we recorded the freight of the goods purchased. In January 4, we decreased the amount of payable with the amount of goods returned. As can be noticed, the rules in debit and credit are fairly the same. Purchases is an expense account; thus, it is debited when it occurred. The same is true with Freight In. Purchase Returns, however, is a contra-expense account, thus it is credited when it occurred.

If we are asked how much net purchases were, we can use the formula indicated earlier:

$$\text{Net Purchases} = \text{Purchases} + \text{Freight in} - \text{Purchase Returns} - \text{Purchase Discounts}$$
$$= 20,000 + 750 - 1000$$
$$= 19,750$$

If we assume that there is no beginning inventory, and an inventory end of P4,000, we can compute cost of sales by using the formula as indicated below:

$$\text{Cost of Sales} = \text{Inventory, beginning} + \text{Net Purchases} - \text{Inventory, end}$$
$$= 0 + 19,750 - 4,000$$
$$= 15,750$$

To compute for cost of sales for the period using the report format as also indicated earlier, we get the following:

Cost of Sales		
Inventory, beginning		-
Add: Net Purchases		
Purchases	20,000.00	
Add: Freight In	750.00	
Total	20,750.00	
Less: Purchase Returns	1,000.00	
Purchase Discounts	-	19,750.00
Total Goods Available		19,750.00
Less: Inventory, end		4,000.00
Cost of Sales		**15,750.00**

The foregoing discussions are just illustrations for purposes of acquainting ourselves with transactions affecting restaurants. A sample of an income statement of a hotel which offers several services, including a restaurant, is shown below:

	Resort	Restaurant	TOTAL
Income			
4100 · Accommodation Income	3,062,554.80	0.00	3,062,554.80
4120 · Ministore Sales	12,354.00	0.00	12,354.00
4200 · Restaurant Income	0.00	2,025,531.33	2,025,531.33
4300 · Service Revenue	135,992.50	0.00	135,992.50
4400 · Rental Revenue	55,400.00	0.00	55,400.00
4500 · Communications Revenue	1,256.00	0.00	1,256.00
4600 · Commission Revenue	9,730.00	0.00	9,730.00
Total Income	3,277,287.30	2,025,531.33	5,302,818.63
Cost of Goods Sold			
5000 · Cost of Goods Sold	0.00	816,967.53	816,967.53
Total COGS	0.00	816,967.53	816,967.53
Gross Profit	3,277,287.30	1,208,563.80	4,485,851.10
Expense			
5041 · FOC-meals	137,997.56	14,686.40	152,683.96
5042 · Staff meals	36,080.00	36,160.00	72,240.00
5100 · Room Supplies	31,846.90	0.00	31,846.90
5115 · Ministore	10,443.50	0.00	10,443.50
5200 · Salaries & Wages	326,520.75	468,735.28	795,256.03
5250 · SSS/PHIC/PAGIBIG	19,829.10	18,359.70	38,188.80
5300 · Employee Benefits	25,812.10	39,734.88	65,546.98
5400 · Maintenance/Repairs	204,743.34	95,463.25	300,206.59
5500 · Communication Expense	27,915.32	800.00	28,715.32
5550 · Utilities Expense	138,345.09	84,526.53	222,871.62
5600 · Office Expenses	38,408.75	0.00	38,408.75
5700 · Front Office Supplies	21,016.00	0.00	21,016.00
5750 · Taxes & Licenses	58,078.10	17,281.98	75,360.08
5760 · Insurance Expense	1,584.40	1,936.92	3,521.32
5800 · Rent Expense	32,850.00	0.00	32,850.00
5850 · Promotions & Advertising	49,878.32	0.00	49,878.32
5900 · Contracted Services	67,362.50	0.00	67,362.50

5950 · Commission Expense	150.00	0.00	150.00
6000 · Administrative Expenses	13,741.66	0.00	13,741.66
6050 · Service Charge-Credit Cards	3,912.62	23,974.28	27,886.90
Total Expense	1,246,516.01	801,659.22	2,048,175.23
Net Income	**2,030,771.29**	**406,904.58**	**2,437,675.87**

Other Accounting Reports for Hotels and Restaurants

We list below other reports that are normally prepared by hotels and restaurants:

a. Occupancy Report – this tells us of the occupancy details of the hotel and shows the computation for occupancy rate (rooms occupied divided by total number of available rooms). It may also summarize the nature of bookings of a particular period of time. An example is show below:

Data Summary:

Total Number of Guests for the Month	81
Total Number of Occupied Room Nights*	329
Occupancy Rate	97.9%

Note: Occupied room nights include 2 nights considered sold

Total guestroom nights is 12.

Guest Profile by Class Type:

	Number	%
Local Residents	17	21%
Foreigners	64	79%
TOTAL	81	100%

Guest Profile by Nature of Accommodation:

	Number	%
Walk-in	5	6%
Direct Booking	41	51%
Agency Assisted	35	43%
TOTAL	81	100%

Guest Profile by Country of Origin:

Country	Number	Rank	%
Local Residents			
Philippines	7		9%
Japan	3		4%
Others*	7		9%

Guest Profile by Length of Stay:

Length of Stay*	Number	%
13 nights	1	1%
12 nights	0	0%
11 nights	0	0%

b. Bar Inventory Report – tracks the inventory of the previous day and compares it with current day inventory to investigate discrepancies or irregularities. An example is presented on the next page:

Item	Prior Day Inventory	This Day's Inventory	Remarks
Fernet Branca, 100cl	1 bottle and 1680 g on February 18	1680 g on February 19	No sale for one bottle is recorded, cannot be traced
Jim Beam Gold, 750 ml	1 bottle and 517 g on February 24	517 g on February 25	No sale for one bottle recorded, cannot be traced
Cinzano Bianco	1 bottle and 850 g on February 24	850 g on February 25	No sale for one bottle recorded, cannot be traced.

c. Daily F & B Revenue Report – a report that shows the daily sales of the food and beverage department (restaurant and bars) segregated according to source or type.

JANUARY OS No.	Cash	Room charge	Credit Card	Villa Package	KH Package	Credit	FOC	Food	Beverage	Minibar Food
RESTAURANT										
37731				900.00				900.00		
37732				900.00				900.00		
37733		270.00						200.00	70.00	
37734				900.00				900.00		
37735				900.00				900.00		
37736				900.00				900.00		
37737				1,350.00				1,350.00		
37738		330.00							330.00	
37739		930.00						930.00		
37740				900.00				900.00		
37741				900.00				900.00		
37742	500.00							450.00	50.00	
37743	460.00							310.00	150.00	
37744		950.00						760.00	190.00	
37745							340.00			
37746							460.00			
37747							650.00			
37748		390.00							390.00	

d. Daily Other Income Report – shows the daily revenue receipts of other income sources of the resort. This includes, among others, revenues from ministore, transfers, telephone, and other related sources.

DATE	CASH	CREDIT CARD	ROOM CHARGE	MINISTORE	TRANFERS	PHOTO COPY	TEL. F.O.	LAUNDRY	POOL	SUNBED	PING PONG
1-Apr	2,370.00	-	1,500.00	300.00	-	20.00	-	-	1,200.00	750.00	-
2-Apr	2,402.00	-	847.00	190.00	-	24.00	-	385.00	1,100.00	1,000.00	-
3-Apr	6,907.00	-	1,013.00	1,290.00	980.00	-	-	-	400.00	2,250.00	-
4-Apr	1,189.00	-	1,515.00	309.00	-	-	-	1,045.00	-	750.00	150.00
5-Apr	1,780.00	-	2,452.00	502.00	1,360.00	30.00	-	590.00	400.00	1,250.00	-
6-Apr	4,631.00	-	581.00	1,062.00	-	-	-	-	2,000.00	1,250.00	-
7-Apr	3,955.00	2,800.00	2,294.00	383.00	980.00	-	-	-	5,236.00	1,000.00	-
8-Apr	1,976.00	-	-	340.00	-	36.00	-	-	1,000.00	500.00	-
18-Feb	2,956.00	-	2,455.00	1,220.00	680.00	56.00	-	885.00	2,400.00	500.00	-
10-Apr	900.00	-	3,495.00	305.00	1,360.00	-	-	1,830.00	400.00	500.00	-
11-Apr	3,278.00	-	610.00	304.00	-	24.00	-	510.00	-	1,250.00	-
12-Apr	952.00	-	731.00	383.00	-	-	-	-	800.00	-	-
13-Apr	2,009.00	-	350.00	509.00	-	-	50.00	-	1,800.00	-	-
14-Apr	2,150.00	-	79.00	129.00	-	-	-	-	2,000.00	-	-

e. Daily Inventory Report – This report shows the movement of the inventory on a daily basis and includes the analysis of consumption of inventory with corresponding costs.

28-Feb	STOCK					COST PRICE	new	Ending
ITEMS	OPEN	FORWARD	CLOSE	ISSUE		PER UNIT	PER PORTION	S. PRICE	Balance
LIQUORS & SCHNAPS									
ABSINTHE	1264	1264	1264		750	2,000.00	66.67	240.00	404.48
AMARETTO DISARONNO	867	867	867		750	860.00	28.67	240.00	277.44
AMARETTO CLASSICO	515	515	515		700	700.00	25.00	240.00	176.57
APRICOT BRANDY	648	648	648		750	270.00	9.00	20.00	17.28
BAILEYS CREAM 750 ml	790	790	790		750	688.50	22.95	240.00	252.80
BENEDICTINE	1349	1349	1349		700	525.00	18.75	240.00	462.51
BLUE CURACAO	653	653	653		700	1,069.00	38.18	20.00	18.66
BRANCA MENTA	897	897	897		750	835.00	27.83	20.00	23.92
CHERRY BRANDY	803	803	769		750	347.00	11.57	20.00	20.51
CACHACA	1307	1307	1307		1,000	780.00	19.50	20.00	26.14
COINTREAU	882	882	882		750	940.00	31.33	240.00	282.24
CREME DE BANANES	670	670	670		750	250.00	8.33	20.00	17.87
CREME DE CACAO brown	1085	1085	1085		750	250.00	8.33	20.00	28.93
CREME DE CACAO white	1129	1129	1129		750	250.00	8.33	20.00	30.11
CREME DE MENTHE green	925	925	925		750	250.00	8.33	20.00	24.67

f. Monthly Salary Summary – shows the monthly salary summary of the hotel segregated as to revenue source. In the example below, note that accounting and administrative employees, for example, are charged accordingly to the department where they work.

Summary of Salaries Expense per Revenue Source
For the month of February 2010

	1st half	2nd half	Total
Accounting and Admin Employees			
1 A	4,928.34	4,389.00	9,317.34
2 B	5,137.03	4,904.25	10,041.28
3 C	4,290.00	4,620.00	8,910.00
4 D	3,120.00	3,120.00	6,240.00
5 E	2,413.00	2,137.00	4,550.00
6 F	4,470.00	5,854.16	10,324.16
7 G	4,022.58	4,077.81	8,100.39
charged to resort	28,380.95	29,102.22	57,483.17
			-
1 X	3,860.16	3,648.44	7,508.60
2 Y	3,392.81	3,439.81	6,832.62
3 Z	2,227.97	2,403.41	4,631.38
charged to restaurant	9,480.94	9,491.66	18,972.60
			-
	37,861.89	38,593.88	76,455.77
Kitchen			
1 Q	3,525.38	4,625.62	8,151.00
2 R	1,691.16	2,406.66	4,097.82
3 S	2,535.91	2,818.11	5,354.02
4 Y	3,525.38	4,007.48	7,532.86
5 U	1,633.53	1,940.25	3,573.78

g. Monthly Time Record Summary – presents the total days worked by employee, with details of overtime and undertime. This is the basis for the computation of the monthly payroll.

		WAITERS AND BARTENDERS							
		A	B	C	D	E	F	G	h
TOTAL	over/under TIM	19.87	(1.68)	(6.08)	0.67	1.17	24.22	(3.83)	(0.47)
	no. of days	12	13	12	13	15	14	14	14

These are just a few of the accounting and financial reports prepared for hotels and restaurants. These are presented to give the reader an idea of the different reports prepared for these establishments.

End of Chapter Exercises

Exercise 8.1

Name:	Course &year:	Date:
Subject:	Time:	Score:

Discussion Questions. Individually, or in groups, answer the following questions:

1. How similar or different is accounting for hotels from other service-concern establishments?

2. What new things did you learn in this chapter that is significantly different from those you learned in the previous discussions?

3. What do you think is the revenue driver (that which causes the revenue accounts to increase) for both hotels and restaurants? Why?

4. Why do you think is it necessary to account separately for the revenue of each type of service offered by hotels?

5. In the case of hotels, what do you think is its largest expense? Why?

Exercise 8.2

Name:	Course &year:	Date:
Subject:	Time:	Score:

Multiple Choice. Encircle the letter of the answer that corresponds to your choice.

1. Which of the following is not an auxiliary source of revenue for hotels?
a. minibar   b) mini-store c) room service   d) telephone   e) none of these

2. A hotel business
a. Provides services to the public
b. Offers accommodation to guests
c. Offers auxiliary services apart from accommodation
d. All of the responses

3. Which of the following statements is true?
a. Trade discounts are given to further trade
b. Trade discounts are recorded in the books of accounts
c. Trade discounts are deducted from invoice price
d. All of the responses

4. Abiabi Hotel sold one room on account. This transaction will affect the
a. Balance sheet only   c) balance sheet and income statement
b. Income statement only   d) balance sheet, income statement,
                                            And statement of capital

5. When gross profit is deducted with operating expenses, the answer is
a) net sales   c) net income
b) merchandise inventory, beginning   d) purchases

6. A restaurant normally sells food and beverages. As such the restaurant is considered a
a) merchandising business   c) manufacturing business
b) mixed business   d) service business

7. Which of the following room sales is not collected from the personal account of guests?
a. Direct-booking   c) walk-in
b. Agency-assisted   d) none of these

8. In the term "20% off on all beverages", 20% means
a) discount   c) due date
b) return   d) rate

9. Which of the following is not considered income to the restaurant
a) dine-in sales   c) beverage sales
b) corkage fees   d) tip

10. Which of the following is not considered part of food cost?
a) kitchen worker's salaries   c) table napkins
b) fuel   d) none of these

11. What type of business is a hotel?
a. manufacturing   b. trading   c. service   d. none of these

12. A guest who does not have a prior-arranged booking with the hotel
a. walk-in   b. direct-booking   c. agency-assisted   d. none of these

13. Occupancy rate refers to
a. the number of booked rooms divided by the number of available rooms
b. the number of rooms available divided by the total number of rooms
c. the number of rooms occupied by guests divided by the total number of rooms
d. the number of rooms occupied by guests divided by the number of billed rooms

14. In agency assisted sales, the one who has the obligation to pay the hotel is the
a. guest   b. credit card company   c. travel agency   d. none of these

15. Which of the following is an asset peculiar to hotels
a. furniture   b. land   c. linens, towels and curtains   d. building

16. All of the following offer almost the same kind/nature of product except
a. restaurant   b. bed and breakfast   c. pension house   d. resort

17. A document proving a prior-arranged booking of a guest with the travel agent
indicating the name of the resort, the name of guests, and the number of booked nights
a. official receipt   b. sales invoice   c. voucher   d. none of these

18. Which is a main source of hotel revenue?
a. rental   b. accommodation   c. minibar   d. laundry and pressing

19. For hotels and resorts, rental, minibar, mini-store, and massage are considered what
type of income?
a. accessory   b. ancillary   c. auxiliary   d. none of these

20. The account debited when a guest occupies a room booked through a travel agent
a. cash   b. AR-guest   c. AR-credit card   d. AR- travel agent

Exercise 8.3

Name:	Course &year:	Date:
Subject:	Time:	Score:

True or False: On the blanks provided, write TRUE if the statement is true and FALSE if otherwise.

1. The normal balance of Sales account is credit.

   ____

2. The normal balance of Purchases account is debit.

   ____

3. Restaurants normally use the cost-plus system in computing prices.

   ____

4. Inventory end becomes inventory beginning in the following month.

   ____

5. Freight in is the handling charges for goods sold.

   ____

6. Tip to waiters is considered a revenue for restaurants.

   ____

7. In setting up prices for restaurants, a balance between quantity and price must be achieved.

   ____

8. When a room is sold through an agent, only balance sheet accounts are affected.

   ____

9. When a restaurant customer pays through cash, only income statement accounts are affected.

   ____

10. When cost of goods available for sale is deducted with ending inventory, the result is gross profit.

    ____

Exercise 8.4

Name:	Course &year:	Date:
Subject:	Time:	Score:

Problem Solving. Solve for the required amounts in each of the given problem.

1. The following data were presented for Wanton Restaurant, as lifted from the books of accounts: Merchandise inventory, October 1, P151, 000; Purchases, P427, 000; Freight-in, P8, 500; Purchases Returns and Allowances, P2, 000; Purchase Discount, P5, 000; Sales, P590, 000; Sales Returns and Allowances, P1, 500; Sales Discount, P8, 000; Freight-in, P1, 800; Merchandise Inventory, October 31, P170, 000.

Required:
   a. Net sales
   b. Net Purchases
   c. Cost of sales
   d. Gross Profit
   e. Net Income

2. The following data relates to Whatever Resto:
Sales – P620,000, Sales Returns – P8,000, Sales Discounts –P12,000, Purchases – P890,000, Purchase Discounts – P20,000, Freight In – P16,000, Beginning Inventory – P340,000, Ending Inventory – P280,000, Salaries Expense – P78,000, Business Taxes – P12,600, Rent Expense –P15,500, Utilities Expense – P16,500, Telephone Expense – P5,670.

Compute for:
   a. Net Sales
   b. Net Purchases
   c. Cost of Sales
   d. Gross Profit
   e. Net income

3. Compute for missing items

	A	B	C
Sales	P245,000	P_______	P700,000
Beginning Inventory	32,000	36,000	60,000
Purchases	89,000	_______	_______
Ending Inventory	43,000	240,000	70,000
Cost of Goods Sold	_______	80,000	_______

		110,000	280,000
Gross Income		110,000	280,000
Operating Expenses	66,000		40,000
Net Income (Net Loss)	12,000	18,000	

Exercise 8.5

Name:	Course &year:	Date:
Subject:	Time:	Score:

Journalizing – Hotel Business. Journalize the following transactions. Use journal sheets.

Mr. Max Abiabi opened a pension house called Abiabi Pension House. The following business transactions were completed for the month of May 2008. Room rates for the whole month was P1,000 per room per night.

May   1   Mr. Abiabi invested the following:

                   Cash   P200, 000.00

                   Land and Building   500,000.00

      3   Bought room supplies P5,000 and linens and curtains P12,000 on account

      5   Purchased furniture and fixtures P50,000.00 and paid cash

      6   Paid business permits, P6750

      7   Four guests arrived without booking. They stayed for one night in separate rooms and paid cash in full.

      8   Paid one half of its payable on May 3

      9   Made a loan from the bank, P50,000

    18   Paid P9,000 for workers' salaries

    19   One guest arrived with a travel voucher from an agent. He would stay for 2 nights.

    19   The three guests on May 16 checked out and paid their accounts in full

    20   Mr. Abiabi made a cash withdrawal of P4000.00

    27   One guest arrived to stay for one night. He paid his account in full and asked for his pair of pants to be washed. The front desk charged the guest P150. These are all paid in cash.

    28   Paid light and water bills P5,650

    30   Paid salaries of workers, P2,500

The following chart of account is presented.

Cash	Loans Payable
Accounts Receivable-Guest	Abiabi, Capital
Accounts Receivable-Travel Agent	Abiabi, Drawing
Accounts Receivable- Credit Card	Accommodation Income
Room Supplies	Laundry Income
Land and Building	Salaries and Wages
Room Furniture	
Linens and Curtains	Taxes and Licenses
Accounts Payable	Utilities Expense

Exercise 8.6

Name:	Course &year:	Date:
Subject:	Time:	Score:

Trial Balance and Financial Statements Preparation for Hotel Business. Prepare a trial balance, income statement, and balance sheet given the following ledger balances of Pahiyum Bed and Breakfast for the month May 2018.

Cash - P1,152,000; Accounts Receivable – Travel Agents – P34,000; Room Supplies Inventory – P40,000; Building – P2,294,000; Loans Payable – P240,000; Pahiyum Capital – P3,200,000; Pahiyum, Drawing – 100,000; Accommodation Income – P323,000; Wages Expense – P63,000; Transportation Expense – P40,000; Advertising Expense – P18,000; Utilities Expense – P22,000.

Exercise 8.7

Name:	Course &year:	Date:
Subject:	Time:	Score:

Journalizing – Restaurant Business. Journalize the following transactions. Use journal sheets.

Tuna Deli has the following transactions in May 2088

1	Owner invested cash in the business, P500,000, Kitchen Equipment P2,000,000 and tables and chairs for P400,000
2	Purchased restaurant supplies on account from Napkins Co. P15000
3	Purchased canned goods, sausages, etc from Sausage Co. P85,000 for cash
4	Returned defective merchandise to Napkins Co. P1,000
5	Paid the amount due to Napkins Bought rice, pasta, and other goods from Risotto, P25000
6	Paid business permits, P2,500
8	Restaurant sales for the week, P12,000 for cash, P2,000 on account
11	Purchased spices from Onions Company, P4,200
13	Paid freight for goods purchased from Onions, P420
14	Restaurant sales for the week, P5,450 cash, P4,250 on account
15	Paid salaries to workers, P24,000
16	Purchased vegetables and other perishables from Rosales, P12,000 for cash
19	Collected in full the accounts on May 8
22	Paid light and water bills, P4500
23	Owner withdrew cash from the business – P5000
24	Sales for the week, P15,000 for cash, P2,000 on account
28	Purchased vegetables, meat from Rosales, P14,500 on account
29	Collected in full the accounts on May 14
30	Paid salaries of workers, P23,800

Note: Restaurant Inventory on January 31, 2008 was P14,600.

Required: Record the following transactions and prepare the trial balance, statement of financial operations, statement of changes in equity, and statement of financial position. Use the following account titles:

Cash	Sales	Supplies Expense
Accounts Receivable	Sales Discount	Taxes and Licenses
Restaurant Inventory	Purchases	Salaries and Wages
Equipment	Purchase Return	Light and Water
Furniture and Fixtures	Freight in	
Tuna, Capital		
Tuna, Drawing		

Exercise 8.8

Name:	Course &year:	Date:
Subject:	Time:	Score:

Trial Balance and Financial Statements Preparation for Restaurant Business. Prepare a trial balance, income statement, and balance sheet given the following ledger balances of Pahiyum Bed and Breakfast for the month April 2018.

Solo Resto
30 April 2018
Trial Balance

	Dr	Cr
Cash in Bank	216,000.00	
Accounts Receivable	142,500.00	
Restaurant Inventory, April 1	786,265.00	
Linens	24,000.00	
Unused Supplies	17,829.00	
Furniture and Fixtures	350,000.00	
Equipment	72,500.00	
Other Assets	12,260.00	
Accounts Payable		299,156.00
Loans Payable		350,000.00
Notes Payable		100,000.00
Solo, Capital		1,250,000.00
Solo, Drawing	26,500.00	
Sales		3,126,555.00
Sales Discounts	12,569.00	
Purchases	2,989,560.00	
Purchase Returns		5,560.00
Freight in	12,900.00	
Salaries Expense	378,958.00	

Light and Water	85,365.00	
Taxes and Licenses	475.00	
Interest Expense	3,590.00	
TOTALS	5,131,271.00	5,131,271.00

Inventory as of April 30 amounted to P1,356,822

Bibliography

Ainsworth, Penne and Dan Deines. *Introduction to Accounting: An Integrated Approach* New York: McGraw-Hill/Irwin, 2016.

Bazley, John D., Loren A. Nikolai, Jefferson P. Jones. *Intermediate Accounting 11th edition*. USA: Southwestern Cengage Learning, 2010.

Beg, M.A., Manoj K. Dash. *Managerial Economics*. United Kingdom: Global Professional Publishing Ltd, 2010.

Brue, Stanley L., Campbell R. McConnell, Sean M. Flynn. *Essentials of Economics 3rd edition*. New York: McGraw-Hill/Irwin, 2013.

Cabrera, Ma Elenita B., Ester Francisco Ledesma, Ma. Conception Lupisan. *Fundamentals of Accounting Vol. 1 , 2010 edition*. Manila, Philippines: GIC Enterprises & Co., INC., 2010.

Case, Karl E., Ray C. Fair, Sharon Oster. *Principles of Economics 11th edition*. Philippines: Pearson Education Asia PTE.LTD, 2017.

Cox, Simon, Ed. *Economics: Making Sense of the Modern Economy*. London: Profile Books Ltd., 2006

De Leon, Hector S. *The Law of Partnership and Private Corporations*. Manila, Philippines: Rex Bookstore, 2013.

Daft, Richard L. *Management 12th edition*. Boston: CEngage, 2015.

Edmonds, Thomas P., Philip R. Olds, Frances M. McNair, Bor-Yi Tsay.*Survey of Accounting 4th edition*. New York: Mc-Graw-Hill Co. Inc., 2014.

Gitman, Lawrence and Zutter, Chad. *Principles of Managerial Finance. 13th Edition.* Boston: Prentice Hall. 2012.

Horngren, Charles, Datar, Srikant, and Rajan Madhav. *Cost Accounting: Concepts and Practices 15th edition*. London: Pearson Education. 2015.

Hurt, Robert L. *Accounting Information Systems; Basic Concepts and Current Issues 4th edition*. New York: Mcgraw-Hill, 2016.

Jeter, Debra C. and Paul K. Chaney. *Advance accounting 6th edition*. New Jersey: John Wiley & Sons Pte Ltd., 2014.

Kieso, Donald E., Jerry J. Weygandt, Terry D. Warfield. *Intermediate Accounting 16th edition*. New Jersey: John Wiley & Sons (Asia) Pte Ltd, 2016.

Kimwell, Mercedes Bartolome. *Constructive Accounting 6th edition*. Manila, Philippines: GIC Enterprises & Co., INC., 2007

Larson, Kermit D., John J. Wild, Barbara Chiappetta. *Principles of Financial Accounting 17th edition*. New York: McGraw-Hill Education, 2005.

Lopez, Rafael M. *Fundamentals of Accounting: Simplified Approach & Procedures Millennial Edition*. Davao City, Philippines: MS Lopez Printing, 2008.

Valix, Conrado T., Jose F. Peralta, Christian Aris M. Valix. *Financial Accounting Vol. 1*. Manila, Philippines: GIC Enterprises & Co., INC., 2009.

Valix, Conrado T., Jose F.Peralta, Christian Aris M. Valix. *Financial Accounting Vol.1*. Manila, Philipines: GIC Enterprises & Co., INC., 2010.

Weygandt, Jerry J., Paul D. Kimmel, Donald E. Kieso. *Accounting Principles 12th edition*. New Jersey: John Wiley & Sons,Inc., 2015.